THE POWER OF PLAY

THE GAME DESIGN APPROACH TO TRANSFORMING EMPLOYEE ENGAGEMENT

GEORGE KESSELMAN

WILEY

This edition first published 2024

George Kesselman © 2024

Registered Office(s)
John Wiley & Sons, Inc., 111 River Street, Hoboken, NJ 07030, USA

John Wiley & Sons Ltd, The Atrium, Southern Gate, Chichester, West Sussex, PO19 8SQ, UK

Editorial Office
The Atrium, Southern Gate, Chichester, West Sussex, PO19 8SQ, UK

For details of our global editorial offices, customer services, and more information about Wiley products visit us at www.wiley.com.

Wiley also publishes its books in a variety of electronic formats and by print-on-demand. Some content that appears in standard print versions of this book may not be available in other formats. Designations used by companies to distinguish their products are often claimed as trademarks. All brand names and product names used in this book are trade names, service marks, trademarks or registered trademarks of their respective owners. The publisher is not associated with any product or vendor mentioned in this book.

Library of Congress Cataloging-in-Publication Data is Available:

ISBN 9781394228010 (Hardback)
ISBN 9781394230761 (ePDF)
ISBN 9781394230754 (ePub)

Cover Design: Wiley
Cover Image: © Vasyl Onyskiv/AdobeStock
Author Photo: Courtesy of the Author

SKY10057933_102023

This book is lovingly dedicated to my extraordinary wife, who, against all odds, continues to stand by my side, championing my seemingly wild ideas, even when they steer beyond her expectations.

To my children, who occasionally yearn for more shared moments with their dad, yet never cease to show understanding and patience toward my pursuits.

And to my father, who fostered my growth, providing me with the time and space to evolve, and tirelessly shielded me from life's many adversities.

You are the lights guiding my path, the pillars of strength that fuel my endeavors. You inspire me to stretch my boundaries, to continually strive for more.

With my utmost gratitude.

CONTENTS

CONTENTS

PREFACE

Have you ever plunged into the immersive world of a video game, only to re-emerge and find that time has run away from you? Hours evaporated into thin air, daylight surrendered to the velvet cloak of the night, and all while you remained lost in your virtual reality. You were in the zone, fully and utterly captivated by the mission at hand.

Games are more than mere distractions or sources of entertainment. Their allure resides in the carefully orchestrated elements that resonate with our intrinsic motivations—challenge, mastery, exploration, and connection.

The exhilaration that swells in your chest when you conquer a level, the satisfaction humming in your veins when you decode a particularly tricky puzzle, or the warmth spreading through you when you collaborate with your fellow players— all of these feelings spring from a well-designed game.

Now, consider your work. Is it as enthralling as a game? Do you feel that same exhilaration, satisfaction, and warmth? Or has the word "work" become synonymous with monotony and dread? This contrast between our experiences of work and gaming is not inevitable—it is the product of design.

PREFACE

Work, much like a game, can be engineered to be fun and inspiring, if it appeals to our core motivations. If we could draw inspiration from the same playbook that game designers have mastered, we could transform our workplaces into arenas that foster the same kind of engagement, satisfaction, and productivity.

This book is an exploration into that possibility. It serves as a beacon to guide us out of the age-old paradigms of work, and into a future where work does not just coexist with fun—it becomes fun. It aims to unravel the secret behind the appeal of games and to present a practical, actionable strategy to inject that same appeal into the fabric of work. Together, we'll delve into the gaming philosophies that could form the blueprint for the future of work. Welcome, Player One. It's time to reimagine work.

INTRODUCTION: LET'S PRESS START

There's a sobering reality that we all have to face: we spend a staggering 90,000 hours of our lives at work, according to some estimates.[1] Yet, we're far from content, with dissatisfaction echoing in our cubicles, Zoom calls, and home offices. You and I, the chances are, part of the same majority—the 80% who report feeling disengaged, even despondent, at work. This unhappiness doesn't remain confined within the boundaries of our 9 to 5, it seeps into every corner of our lives.

A 2022 Gallup study provided a stark picture: a mere 21% of employees worldwide feel truly engaged in their work.[2] This statistic underscores an urgent imperative to rethink not just where work happens, but how. These trends have been on an upward trajectory, and like a merciless tide, the COVID-19 pandemic swept in, further exposing and accelerating them.

If you're among the fortunate few who feel joyful and engaged at work, consider yourself lucky. But even then, this book will serve as a valuable roadmap to understand why the majority of your colleagues and teammates bear such an oppressive burden when it comes to work. It will provide insights into how we can elevate the work experience, starting with a few simple tweaks.

In today's world, it seems almost universal to assume that work is, by its very nature, a grind—something tedious, daunting, and often, downright dreadful. The paycheck at the end of the month seems like compensation for the daily toll of monotony and disenchantment we endure. It is as though we are marching on an endless treadmill, driven by the ceaseless narrative that this is simply how work "works."

So why, then, have 34% of American adults—the equivalent of 56.4 million people—awakened to the allure of side gigs, a figure that has nearly quadrupled over the course of just three years since the pre-COVID era? What is behind this seismic shift, and how did it come to be?

But here is the real question: What if we've been looking at work through the wrong lens all along? What if our collective understanding of work is flawed, and there exists a more fulfilling, engaging way to labor? And what if this fresh perspective on work could lead us to a more rewarding life today, rather than perpetually deferring our happiness to a distant, elusive retirement, be it early or at the conventional age?

A question flickered insistently in my mind like a neon sign as I gazed blankly at the relentless cascade of emails on my laptop screen one Monday afternoon in January 2022. A deluge of urgent requests from clients, teams, and partners, the digital embodiment of my role as the Chief Commercial

Officer of a fast-growing Asian unicorn, a startup boasting an exclusive billion-dollar valuation club membership. I had scaled the peak of my second career pinnacle, yet, ironically, I was not "loving it"—a phrase conspicuously missing from my work-life lexicon, contrary to the promise of the myriad career guides and corporate propaganda.

Theoretically, I had all the makings of a successful career—a comfortable salary, a prestigious title, and substantial responsibilities. But instead of experiencing the promised euphoria, I found myself submerged in a quagmire of dread and dissatisfaction. Was I wired differently, an anomaly, a statistical outlier in the distribution of work-related happiness? Or was this dissatisfaction indicative of a more fundamental, systemic issue?

Having wrapped up another indistinguishable day of work, I decided to embark on a lengthy, reflective walk. It was not just an ordinary stroll; it was a journey through the labyrinth of my thoughts, an introspective quest for clarity. Such walks had always proved therapeutic when I found myself standing at the crossroads.

My thoughts journeyed back a few years when, as one of the youngest country Chief Operating Officers at an American Insurance Group, I managed a formidable team of over 150 finance and operations professionals across Indonesia and Malaysia. In retrospect, it was evident that I had navigated various forms of work: first, as a student, then as a young professional in Canadian startups, and now, as a key executive in a prominent organization.

A considerable chunk of this work was repetitive, unenjoyable, and at times, utterly pointless. Yet, it was all packaged under the premise that such work was the path to success—a nebulous concept that often amounted to a fat bank balance and ample free time to revel in luxury. This promised oasis of success always seemed just a step away, yet the gap seemed eternal.

Post-reflection, the monotonous grind of the workweek appeared even more baffling. The 40-hour routine seemed an outdated vestige from the industrial revolution era, an inefficient relic of the past. And so, I headed home, my mind teeming with these unresolved thoughts over a hastily consumed dinner.

With my intellectual progress at an impasse, I turned to an alternate universe for solace. My PlayStation beckoned, and I plunged into the exhilarating chaos of Grand Theft Auto. As I embarked on my next challenging mission, I found myself engrossed in the game, my mind electrified. Four hours of virtual adventure later, I was ready to retire for the night. However, a thought flickered in the recesses of my mind: could the answer to my existential question about work lie within the realm of these games?

Unbeknownst to me then, the answer to my career conundrum was lurking in a realm far removed from work. It was a surprising revelation, one that patiently awaited my acknowledgment.

The idea of this book began a decade ago. I had been gradually amassing notes, ideas, and insights through endless conversations with executives, academics, designers, and employees from various industries. Recently, the intensity escalated, and the thesis for this book began to crystallize. The pages of this book are an aggregation of knowledge, research, and insights sourced from North America, Asia, and Europe.

Whether you are a seasoned executive nearing retirement and yearning for meaningful engagement or a fresh graduate trying to decipher the seemingly cryptic work culture, or a mid-career professional questioning the promises of the work world, this book is for you. I hope it answers your queries, sparks curiosity, and provides reassurance that the light at the end of the tunnel is not an oncoming train.

Most importantly, I hope it offers solace to those who have silently contemplated joining the ranks of the "Quietly Quitting." There is, indeed, a better way to work, and together, we'll navigate toward it.

It's easy to feel disillusioned after reading countless advice books and attending expensive seminars that promise enlightenment but offer no tangible solutions. As I penned this book, I was committed to focusing on the two 'W's—WHY and SO-WHAT—with the aim of offering meaningful insights and practical advice to transform your work environment into a more engaging, fun-filled space.

Speaking of fun, do you know what the favorite game of the co-creator of the blockchain concept was? A strange question, perhaps, to pose in a book about work. After all, games and work are generally considered diametrically opposed; games being associated with fun and leisure, while work often equates to the less enjoyable aspects of life. However, there's a surprise waiting in the wings. An unexpected connection between games and work that might just unlock a key to revolutionizing our workspaces.

The co-creator of blockchain found inspiration in a game that led to a technology revolution. Is it possible, then, that our beloved games could unlock a better understanding of our brains and offer a fresh perspective on the outdated narrative of work that we've been adhering to for far too long?

In this book, we will delve into the universal appeal of games and make a surprising revelation: The elements of game design can be applied to work, making it more enjoyable and motivating. Through detailed case studies, interviews with industry pioneers, and research-backed principles, we'll explore how incorporating game design elements can contribute to a work culture of engagement and satisfaction.

Games have always been an integral part of my life. As I grew older, however, societal expectations resulted in an undue guilt associated with gaming. Time spent playing games felt unproductive when it could have been spent working toward financial security and retirement. Games were leisurely Sunday hikes, work was the Monday morning grind. It felt like two separate realms, never meant to intertwine.

Yet, games have a way of immersing us in exciting new worlds, often bringing us closer to friends or allowing us to embark on exhilarating solo adventures. What may seem like mere fun and games hides a deeper secret. The very essence of games, the engagement, challenge, and fun they provide, can be applied to transform the drudgery of work into an enjoyable, fulfilling experience.

By diving into the science of games, we discover that their appeal isn't merely for relaxation. Games stimulate enjoyment, learning, problem-solving, and so much more. They span ages, countries, and backgrounds, and take myriad forms from board games to video games.

You may rightly ask: hasn't this been attempted before? The gamification of work and school, that fell short of expectations. Indeed, the past has seen efforts at gamifying work environments that did not deliver the desired results. But it is precisely these past attempts that provide us valuable insights into what works and what doesn't.

This book aims to uncover the essence of games that makes them so captivating and explores how we can integrate this essence into work, while leaving behind the superficial elements. With a fresh perspective, we are better equipped to understand past attempts and why they may have fallen short.

As I worked on this book, the rapidly evolving world of work became even more evident, especially with the emergence of the next generation of intelligent technologies like Generative AI. The world was both awed and alarmed by the capacity of this AI to perform tasks previously thought exclusive to humans, reigniting fears of an AI-driven future where human jobs become obsolete. This reinforces the urgent need to rethink and reimagine our workspaces.

Work is changing; undergoing a process of "unbundling" as the venture capital industry calls it. Will it happen immediately? Not likely. However, the ways we conduct work over the next two decades will be starkly different from how we have been operating in the past. This transformation will break the stagnation in work efficiency that has plagued us for the last century, bringing about a better working environment for us all.

Throughout this book, we will aim to understand each other better, while also exploring the fascinating world of games— their captivating allure, their challenging nature, and the intriguing fact that we need no compensation to enjoy them.

Did you know that, on average, people around the world spend around 8.5 hours a week playing games? From Singapore to San Francisco, we dedicate nearly a day every week to this enjoyable form of problem-solving. While games are diverse and seemingly endless, they can be categorized into a few types that align with our deep-rooted motivations.

I have always been intrigued by large-scale problems in our environment. They feel like exciting challenges to be solved, similar to games. However, the most complex problems often blend into the backdrop of our lives, becoming nearly invisible as we grow accustomed to their existence. These issues, often overlooked and unaddressed, accumulate over time, leading to substantial challenges. My experience in tackling these challenges at both company and industry levels, along with my curiosity, have given me unique perspectives that I am eager to share with you.

My professional journey has taken me around the world, through various roles in the technology and financial services sectors, eventually leading me to start my own venture, which we successfully sold. My roles have granted me close access to the heart of the action, managing large teams across countries and handling complex office work in support of hundreds of thousands of customers in Indonesia.

The COVID-19 pandemic and its subsequent impact on work have been the catalyst for this book. As we began to recover from the pandemic's effects, it became clear that our approach to work had been fundamentally disrupted. This shift, coupled with newfound freedoms and pressures, has initiated a revolution in how we work.

Having worked with people across various industries and organizational levels, it is evident that the majority of individuals feel disengaged and find work unenjoyable. Traditional thinking has conditioned us to endure this cycle of school and work, collecting societal badges of success, all in the hope of a blissful retirement after 65. However, this narrative is outdated and far from ideal.

Interestingly, our brains are hardwired to enjoy problem-solving and challenges. Some of us thrive in collaborative, bustling environments, while others prefer solitary, quiet spaces. This fact opens up promising possibilities for creating a deeply enjoyable work environment.

Sadly, recent global surveys indicate that only 1 in 10 people in developing countries find their work enjoyable, while the rest feel disengaged.[3] If you're among the fortunate few who enjoy work, this book will offer insights into why you have a positive experience when those around you don't. For the majority who find work stressful and unfulfilling, we'll investigate why work feels so daunting and how we can improve our individual and collective experiences.

While writing and doing research for this book, I often asked people the question: "Does work drain you?" The majority responded with a knowing smile, signaling their shared experience of burnout and its adverse effects, often leading to long-term emotional trauma.

We stand on the brink of a work revolution, promising increased enjoyment, motivation, and engagement, all made possible by the power of game design. This book is an invitation to explore why games are universally loved and how we can apply game design principles to transform our work environment.

In the spirit of best-selling author and a leading authority on motivation, Adam Grant's words, "Let's work together to make work better!" as we embark on this journey. Let's reimagine work, rescue it from the brink of boredom and inefficiency, and strive to create something meaningful and enjoyable. We contemplate how game design principles can inspire a work environment where everyone feels motivated, engaged, and connected. The journey won't be easy, but the destination will be worth it. Let this book be your guide.

There is a better way. It's already happening in pockets of work worldwide, and we are on the verge of a significant shift in how we work. This change will fundamentally alter work's DNA, taking us to a happier place where work accounts for a major part of our lives.

The Structure of the Book

Here's a brief summary to give a glimpse of our upcoming journey together:

- **Part I Work Off:** This introduces the concept of work as a contrast to games.

- **Chapter 1 Trapped in the Cycle: The Woes of Enforced Gamification:** Our journey begins with an exploration of how we became entrapped in our current work patterns and the misery they often cause.

- **Chapters 2–5: The History of Work:** These chapters trace the evolution of work over the last 10,000 years and delve into the influences and approaches that have aimed to improve work, some of which have proven more effective than others.

- **Part II Who Said It Can't Be All Fun and Games?** Here, we'll examine why games are so irresistibly engaging to us. This isn't just about entertainment, but a deeper understanding that could unravel the work conundrum.

- **Chapter 6 Designing Fun: The Magic of Games:** This chapter offers an insight into how our brains function and manipulate us into putting more energy into certain tasks while dreading others. It examines whether happiness is merely an illusion or a biological trick.

We'll also delve into what makes tasks enjoyable and how our perceptions often mislead us about what will bring us enjoyment. This is addressed as the "early retirement fallacy." Then we discover why toys, games, and platforms like YouTube are so engaging and yet bear little resemblance to our perceptions of work.

- **Chapter 7 Games Give Us a Ray of Hope:** Going beyond surface-level elements, we investigate the core of games and their design. A detour into the realm of gambling will reveal how casinos use behavioral design to create engaging experiences. What if slot machines are designed to promote addiction?

- **Chapter 8 Game Time, Game Type:** In this chapter, we find that certain player personalities align with deeper intrinsic motivations and explore how our preferred games and enjoyable aspects of those games can reveal our gaming personality.

- **Part III The Science of Motivation: Chapters 9 and 10** dive into the science of motivation. We'll dissect ineffective approaches to improving work and discuss how the term "gamification" can be misleading and potentially harmful.

- **Part IV The Intersection Between Games and Work: In Chapters 11–13,** we look at parallels with how we learn and take inspiration from open source and esports to see how the right motivation at work can make work enjoyable and engaging.

- **Part V Level-Up Work: Chapters 14–16** synthesize our understanding and envision what this means for the future of work. Three practical strategies to enhance work satisfaction for ourselves and those around us are presented, ranging from immediate changes to long-term boss-level challenges.

We'll apply our newfound knowledge to take the first simple steps toward a future where work is enjoyable and engaging. Most importantly, we'll explore whether work can truly be fun, and fun can be work. I assure you, it will be an eye-opening journey. All that is needed is your curiosity, a love for a good challenge, and an open mind.

Let's dive right in!

Notes

1. A study published in the journal, *Social Science & Medicine*. https://www.sciencedirect.com/science/article/pii/S0277953607001074
2. State of Global Workforce Report by Gallup 2022: "According to the world's workers, not well. Gallup finds 60% of people are emotionally detached at work and 19% are miserable" (p. 2). https://www.gallup.com/workplace/349484/state-of-the-global-workplace.aspx
3. https://www.gartner.com/en/articles/employees-seek-personal-value-and-purpose-at-work-be-prepared-to-deliver

PART I
WORK-OFF:
THE BRIEF HISTORY
OF WORK AND
A SNEAK PEEK
INSIDE OUR HEADS

CHAPTER 1
TRAPPED IN THE CYCLE: THE WOES OF ENFORCED GAMIFICATION

Work life will never return to the pre-pandemic state.
—US Labor Secretary, Marty Walsh[1]

Sarah's story resonated with me when I met her. She was 27 years old and was a few years deep into her tenure at a bank, occupying the prestigious role of a venture investment analyst. Fresh from university, she had battled her way through an intense selection process, emerging victorious to the applause of envious classmates and the approving nods of relatives. Her first few exhilarating months were marked with a generous sign-on bonus and the novelty of a coveted career.

However, as the novelty faded and the monotonous reality of the job seeped in, the thrill transformed into comfort. Around her second year, Sarah noticed a feeling of confinement creeping in, along with a rising tide of demotivation. She chose to persevere, thinking that opportunities like hers were rare. However, the longer she held on, the more drained she felt.

Pursuing a degree in financial technology to propel her career, Sarah found that things were becoming less than hunky-dory. Negative performance reviews came her way, with her manager criticizing her work for failing to meet the bank's standards. The bank responded by enforcing a mandatory training program and setting stringent performance improvement expectations.

Even though Sarah completed the training program, she felt a significant chunk of her remaining freedom was stripped away. Her role had devolved into mechanically following instructions, devoid of any meaningful contribution. Long working hours, coupled with increased pressure and strict expectations, eventually led her to burn out. Despite her sincere efforts, Sarah found herself staring at an even worse performance rating and her first warning letter. She felt desolate, trapped, and powerless.

Such experiences are not uncommon. Like Sarah, many of us might have felt this way or know someone who has. But how does this happen? The answer lies in the concept of learned helplessness, as per behavioral psychologists. This psychological state was a significant factor in Sarah's situation and is crucial to understand how we can reform the concept of work.

Sarah's predicament is not unique, and its roots can be traced back to the structuring of work during the industrial revolution of the eighteenth century. As artisans and craftsmen surrendered their tools and techniques, power shifted dramatically to the factory owners. Individual craftspeople couldn't compete against industrial machines, forcing them to join the production lines. As factory owners possessed the means of production, their power and influence grew, exacerbating the problem of helplessness among the workers.

You might wonder, why would anyone willingly learn helplessness? It's a legitimate question. Let's delve deeper into what learned helplessness is and how it manifests.

Learned helplessness is a psychological state where individuals believe they cannot change their circumstances, leading them not to attempt escaping adverse situations, erecting imaginary barriers in their minds. This is a neurological response, where individuals cease efforts to modify their environment after repeated failures. Over time, their brain reprograms itself, making it harder for them to escape unpleasant situations in the future.

This concept, coined by psychologist Martin Seligman in the late 1960s following controversial studies involving dogs and electric shocks, describes subjects losing hope when confronted with uncontrollable circumstances. In one such experiment, participants were subjected to loud, unpleasant noises, with a lever that might or might not stop the sounds. Participants who couldn't stop the noise in the first round stopped trying to silence it in the subsequent rounds.

In my research, I have interviewed numerous individuals who expressed feeling trapped in their jobs, despite their commitments and high salaries. Does this sound familiar? We enter our first jobs with a sense of excitement and endless possibilities, fueled by big ambitions and ideas. However, we often find ourselves increasingly stuck, doing tasks that lack passion and purpose. We switch jobs repeatedly, hoping to find that magical place of fulfilling work, only to be reminded by bosses, well-intentioned colleagues, and even our parents that such a place may not exist, and we should simply be grateful for having a job that pays the bills.

Learned helplessness is a challenging mindset to overcome, as it involves changes in the brain's structure and function due to repeated stress and negative experiences. Experiencing helplessness triggers the release of stress hormones, such as cortisol, which gradually damages the hippocampus, the region of the brain responsible for learning and memory. This damage impairs the brain's ability to process and store information, further complicating an already difficult situation. As a result, not only do individuals feel trapped in their own narratives, but they also unintentionally reduce their cognitive abilities, effectively throwing away the key to the door to escape.

Furthermore, repeated stress affects the function of the prefrontal cortex, which plays a crucial role in decision-making and executive control. This can lead to a decreased ability to think critically, solve problems, and make decisions, exacerbating feelings of helplessness. It becomes a futile negative spiral.

You might have come across various versions of the story of two frogs, ending up in a milk jug. The story is that the frog that perseveres in pedaling ends up churning milk into butter and jump out while the other one gives up and perishes. While these stories may not be true, they carry a significant lesson. Placing people or frogs in situations where they feel helpless rarely yields positive outcomes. This raises an important question: is helplessness an inherent and inseparable part of work, or is it a negative by-product of the current misstructuring of work?

During a conversation about motivation and work with a financial services executive, who managed a leading company in Singapore, I gained valuable insights that changed my perspective. I asked Mike (not his real name) what he believed was the main motivator for work for most executives. I expected him to mention money, and I was partially correct. However, his answer took an interesting and somewhat surprising angle.

Mike stated that the main motivation for him and his peers was "not to get fired."

His explanation was pragmatic and brutally honest. He went on to elaborate that he received a top salary for making only two or three decisions per week. The rest of his work was designed to keep him occupied and busy, creating the illusion of productivity. In reality, many company teams, such as finance, were only needed around 30% of the time, while the rest of the time was filled with busy work to prevent boredom. This means that, on average, people spend just one day per week on productive work, while the remaining time is spent on superficial tasks to occupy them. Additionally, there is an expectation that they will be available at all times, in an active standby mode, in case something urgent arises.

Mike's story is not an isolated incident; it is far more prevalent than we imagine. According to David Graeber, the author of *Bullshit Jobs: A Theory*,[2] close to 40% of the work we do is unproductive. Work has an interesting characteristic of expanding to fill all available time, much like gas fills a balloon. Software engineers, for example, often share anecdotes about teams given months to solve a problem, spending time on various busy work and failing to produce results, only to have engineers from a different team solve the problem in just two days of focused effort.

Have you ever questioned the purpose of certain tasks assigned to you? It's no wonder we sometimes feel that the work we do is simply make-work projects to keep us occupied.

When I heard these insights, something clicked in my mind, and the inefficiency and inertia of work began to make sense. If we believe that high salaries incentivize organization leaders to deliver the highest value results, we may have it all wrong. Instead, they often focus on avoiding termination, which can lead to building large, inefficient teams working on complex intertwined projects, making themselves irreplaceable. Inefficiency is hidden behind department doors.

During a discussion with the Asia head of HR for a leading financial services firm, she shared a story about her 25-year-old son who works for a tech company in New York. He purposefully disconnects from work at 6 PM every day to prioritize a balanced life. This was a revelation for the head of HR, as her own evenings and weekends were often consumed by overflow work, an accepted part of corporate life. The expectation is that work does not stop when you leave the office. Working long hours, equated with working "hard," becomes a badge of honor and an expectation perpetuated by many leaders who experienced the same grind in their own careers. It quickly becomes a self-fulfilling prophecy, with busy work filling any available time.

In her influential TED talk, "Gaming can make a better world," game designer, researcher, and best-selling author Jane McGonigal[3] emphasized the potential of games as a tool for positive change and creating a better world. She argued that playing games can increase happiness and well-being by providing opportunities for players to feel competent, autonomous, and connected to others.

Gaming offers happiness and fulfillment. McGonigal posits that games tap into our intrinsic motivations by providing settings that are rich with opportunities for achievement, exploration, and relationship building.

However, gamification is only the initial step in exploring the power of games. As best-selling author and a leading authority on motivation, Adam Grant writes in his book, *Originals*,[4] "Games can unlock our inner motivations – beyond extrinsic rewards like money or status – by tapping into intrinsic sources of joy such as curiosity, problem-solving, and creativity." By delving deeper into what games can teach us about our intrinsic motivations, we gain a profound understanding of how to make work more engaging and satisfying. This approach may not be easy, but the effort is undoubtedly worthwhile if it leads to work that is truly fulfilling. By applying the principles of game design, we can create work environments that are both meaningful and enjoyable.

Learned helplessness manifests in various ways within the workplace. Many individuals feel incapable of escaping their jobs or making significant changes in their work lives, perceiving themselves as powerless. Moreover, work often becomes monotonous and unenjoyable, resulting in a sense of hopelessness. Finally, workers frequently experience a constant evaluation and judgment, further reinforcing their feelings of helplessness when it comes to making mistakes.

Before delving deeper into the topic of games, we will explore the demotivators that affect us in the workplace.

The demotivators: unlocking engagement and fulfillment

In her thought-provoking book, *Punished by Rewards*, Alfie Kohn[5] challenges the conventional use of rewards in education, the workplace, and beyond. According to Kohn, rewards create a system of manipulation and external control that undermines intrinsic motivation and causes individuals to focus solely on the reward rather than the joy of the task itself. Instead, Kohn advocates for a supportive environment that fosters autonomy, creativity, and a genuine love of learning.

So, what exactly demotivates us? We asked a diverse range of individuals across industries and countries, and the top three factors were not surprising: (1) a lack of autonomy; (2) feeling unappreciated or unrecognized; and (3) a sense of not contributing to something meaningful or valuable.

When our work offers little to no autonomy, it robs us of our sense of individual control and leaves us feeling powerless. Without the ability to make decisions about our tasks and methods, we lose ownership and agency, resulting in a decline in motivation. Moreover, highly structured and monotonous work strips away our enthusiasm and turns our days into repetitive routines.

But it's not just the work itself. The outdated system of how work is operating (Work Operating System) WorkOS 1.0 treated people as mere cogs in a machine, akin to machines in factories or shops. However, humans are far more complex and capable than linear machines. Treating people like machines is a surefire way to demotivate them and stifle their potential.

Think about a time when you didn't feel appreciated or recognized for your hard work. How did it make you feel? When our contributions go unnoticed or undervalued, our motivation dwindles. Recognition and appreciation are essential for fostering a sense of fulfillment and maintaining our drive to excel.

And what about the bigger picture? Feeling like our work lacks meaning or value can be disheartening. We all crave a sense of purpose and the feeling that our efforts make a difference in the world. When that sense of significance is absent, we start questioning the purpose of our work, leading to a loss of motivation and engagement.

Startlingly, studies show that many individuals feel disengaged or unfulfilled in their work. This not only hampers their ability to solve complex problems but also decreases their productivity and motivation. In fact, the study "Employee Engagement: The Key to Unlocking Potential" by David MacLeod and Nita Clarke[6] reveals that only around 20% of workers are highly engaged, while 60% are moderately engaged and 20% are not engaged at all.

The rise of the gig economy and the increasing flexibility of the workforce further complicate matters. Many gig workers find themselves in short-term or part-time jobs that offer limited opportunities for growth and learning. This hampers their ability to develop the necessary skills and knowledge for tackling complex challenges head-on.

But it's not all doom and gloom. Research suggests that employee engagement is positively associated with job satisfaction, organizational commitment, and performance, while being negatively associated with turnover intentions. This means that engagement is a key ingredient for success, both for individuals and organizations.

It's time to bid farewell to the outdated carrot-and-stick approach and the WorkOS 1.0 that relies on external rewards. They no longer meet the needs of today's complex, knowledge-based work. To unlock true engagement and fulfillment, we must embrace a fundamental upgrade to our WorkOS.

Now, you may be wondering how we can prepare for this transition. It won't happen overnight through a simple workshop or motivational speech. Instead, we are witnessing an unstoppable wave of change sweeping the globe. Companies that resist this shift will find themselves uncomfortable and uncompetitive, gradually fading into oblivion or being absorbed by more progressive organizations.

History teaches us valuable lessons. Companies like Blackberry and Nokia ignored the rising trend of all-screen smartphones, paying a heavy price for their denial in the face of facts and rapid disruption. Similarly, Kodak invented digital film but failed to fully embrace it, fearing the departure from their existing business model.

It's time to break free from the demotivators that hold us back. By fostering autonomy, appreciation, and a sense of purpose in our work, we can unlock engagement, drive, and true fulfillment. It's a journey that requires collective effort, but the rewards are worth it—a future where work is both meaningful and enjoyable awaits us.

Summary

In this chapter, we delved into the concept of learned help-lessness and its implications for work. We explored how the industrial revolution and the shift to factory work contributed to a sense of helplessness among workers.

Learned helplessness was defined as the belief that someone is incapable of altering their situation, leading to a lack of effort to escape aversive situations. We examined the psychological research behind learned helplessness, including the influential studies conducted by psychologist Martin Seligman involving dogs and electric shocks. The findings demonstrated that re-peated exposure to uncontrollable negative experiences can reprogram the brain and make it harder for individuals to es-cape similar situations in the future.

Drawing from real-life examples, we highlighted the experi-ences of individuals like Sarah, who feel trapped and unmoti-vated in their jobs. The damaging effects of learned helplessness on cognitive abilities, such as impaired learning, memory, and decision-making, were explored.

Next, we discussed the demotivators that contribute to a sense of helplessness in the workplace. Lack of autonomy, feeling unappreciated or unrecognized, and a perceived lack of con-tribution to something meaningful were identified as com-mon factors that demotivate individuals.

To provide a broader perspective, we examined the impor-tance of engagement and fulfillment in work. Research indi-cated that a significant number of workers feel disengaged, which can lead to decreased productivity and hinder problem-solving abilities. We also touched on the rise of the gig economy and its impact on skill development and problem-solving capabilities.

Finally, we emphasized the need for a fundamental shift in the way work is structured and approached. The outdated WorkOS 1.0, based on extrinsic rewards and the "carrot-and-stick" approach, was deemed insufficient for the complexities of modern work. Instead, we need to embrace a new WorkOS 2.0 that prioritizes autonomy, creativity, and intrinsic motivation.

The chapter concluded by emphasizing the urgency of this shift and the potential consequences for organizations that fail to adapt. It highlighted the need to prepare for the transition and create a work environment that fosters engagement, fulfillment, and a sense of purpose.

By understanding the impact of learned helplessness and addressing the demotivators in the workplace, we can pave the way for a future where work is not only productive but also enjoyable and meaningful.

Notes

1. https://www.bnnbloomberg.ca/davos-returned-as-a-microcosm-of-workplace-changes-everywhere-1.1875275
2. David Graeber, *Bullshit Jobs: A Theory* (London: Allen Lane, 2018).

3. Jane McGonigal, Gaming can make a better world. TED talk, www.ted.com/talks/jane_mcgonigal_gaming_can_make.
4. Adam Grant, *Originals: How Non-Conformists Move the World* (New York: Viking, 2016).
5. Alfie Kohn, *Punished by Rewards* (Boston: Houghton Mifflin, 1999).
6. David MacLeod and Nita Clarke, Employee engagement: The key to unlocking potential. https://dera.ioe.ac.uk/id/eprint/1810/1/file52215.pdf

CHAPTER 2
THE JOURNEY TO WORK 1.0

The legacy of work: from hours to money

> The factory of the future will have only two employees, a man and a dog. The man will be there to feed the dog. The dog will be there to keep the man from touching the equipment.
> — Warren Bennis

The vast amount of time we spend working in our lives is staggering. On average, we will dedicate nearly 90,000 hours to our jobs, making work a significant portion of our waking hours, second only to sleep. As of 2021, there are approximately 3.3 billion people employed globally, collectively contributing an astonishing 297 trillion hours of work. To put this into perspective, that amount of time is more than double the age of the universe and far surpasses the age of our planet Earth.

Unfortunately, the sad reality is that many people are not satisfied or fulfilled by their work. Gallup's latest research[1] reveals that 60% of individuals are emotionally detached, while 19% are downright miserable in their jobs. This represents not only a significant productivity gap but also a disheartening way to spend a substantial portion of our lives.

Understanding the history of work

The way we work today is a culmination of collective history, generational elements, and powerful narratives that shape our perspectives. To understand how we can break free from the current work paradigm, it is essential to examine the history of work and the driving forces behind its structure.

One of the prime examples that influence our work is the concept of the 40-hour workweek. Although it is now the global standard, the origins of this notion are more practical than scientifically proven. It can be traced back to the late nineteenth century and the Fair Labor Standards Act of 1938 in the United States, which established the 40-hour workweek and minimum wage requirements.

During this era, worker mortality due to exhaustion became a concern, prompting union movements across Europe, particularly in the United Kingdom and France. Workers demanded humane working hours as they endured grueling shifts lasting 12 to 16 hours, seven days a week. The compromise that emerged was the 40-hour workweek, balancing the desire for maximum productivity from factory owners and the need for sustainable working conditions for employees.

The 40-hour workweek was not the result of scientific research but rather a political compromise. Unions sought shorter hours to create more jobs and reduce unemployment, while employers aimed to maintain productivity without reducing workers' pay.

The link between time and money

Another pervasive belief in the realm of work is the notion that higher pay equals higher productivity, alongside the widely held idea that time equals money. This perspective suggests that time is the primary input determining the value we generate, and it has become deeply ingrained in our work culture.

However, the link between time and money is a relatively recent phenomenon in the context of human history. Only around 250 years ago, with the advent of the industrial revolution, did time become the currency of work. The longer a machine operated, the more output and profit it generated for factory owners. People working the machines were expected to keep them fully utilized.

Furthermore, the concept of money as the primary motivator for work is also a relatively recent development. In traditional societies, work was driven by meeting basic survival needs, such as food, shelter, and clothing. Social status and fulfillment held greater importance as motivators than money itself.

With the rise of industrialization and modern capitalism in the nineteenth century, money increasingly became the primary motivator for work. Wages were tied to labor, time committed, or the value of the produced goods. This system of monetary compensation has become the dominant mode of production in many parts of the world, shifting the focus from intrinsic motivators to financial gain. This system is called capitalism.

How did we get there?

It was a bitter, cold morning in February, painting a vivid picture of the hardships faced by working-class individuals in the past. The dim sun barely illuminated the dreary, smoke-filled streets, where tired workers trudged along, blue-fingered and half-frozen, on their way to factories and workshops. Dilapidated houses with cracked walls and broken windows lined the street, while the air was heavy with the scent of rotting garbage. These working men toiled long hours for meager wages, returning home exhausted and dispirited, their homes offering little respite from the harsh realities of their lives.

The year was 1900, and this scene comes from the semi-autobiographical novel, *The Ragged-Trousered Philanthropists*, by Robert Tressell.[2] Through his fictional tale, Tressell shed light on the plight of working-class individuals, chronicling a house painter's struggle to find work and avoid the dreaded workhouse, where survival often meant enduring semi-slavery conditions in exchange for shelter and food.

Work, as we all know it, is a shared experience, regardless of our generation, gender, or background. It is a universal topic that impacts us all. Before delving deeper into the complexities of work, it is important to understand its essence. According to the *Oxford English Dictionary*,[3] work is an activity involving mental or physical effort aimed at achieving a purpose or result. It can refer to a job or occupation, particularly as a means of earning a living. Work is also something that is produced or accomplished through effort, skill, or exertion.

In essence, work encompasses the exertion of physical or mental effort to achieve a specific task or purpose. It encompasses activities that require skill, effort, and dedication to yield the desired outcomes. Work can be compensated or uncompensated, ranging from manual labor to intellectual or creative pursuits. It is the application of energy and effort toward achieving a specific goal or objective.

Exploring the history of work

To understand the present and envision the future of work, we must examine its historical foundations. History provides valuable insights into the evolution of work and the forces that have shaped its current state.

Without a doubt, the past has influenced the present in significant ways. As the saying goes, "Without understanding the past, it is hard to see the future." So, let us embark on a journey through time, unraveling the tapestry of work and uncovering intriguing hints along the way.

By examining the historical context, we can gain a deeper appreciation for the work practices and beliefs that have been passed down through generations. It allows us to question the status quo and explore new possibilities for creating a more fulfilling and meaningful work experience.

Work has come a long way since the days depicted in Tressell's novel, but many challenges and issues still persist. The struggles faced by workers in the past highlight the importance of continually reassessing and evolving our understanding of work.

Work 0.1: Survival and hunter-gatherers

Work, in its most primitive form, can be traced back to the earliest human societies. Our hunter-gatherer predecessors, who roamed the savannas thousands of years ago, engaged in work to sustain their small tribes. Their work consisted of arduous physical effort to catch animals and gather food and resources necessary for survival. It was a highly opportunistic approach, where they exploited the environment lightly, relying on a diverse range of resources.[4]

Life for these early humans was harsh, and the average lifespan was short, estimated to be less than 20 years. Diseases, harsh elements, and limited food availability posed constant challenges. From the moment they could walk, these individuals worked tirelessly to survive, with muscle effort being their primary input. We can refer to this basic, animal-like work as Work 0.1.

Work 1.0: Agriculture, settlements, and specialization

Around 10,000 years ago, the invention of agriculture marked a significant turning point in the history of work. Humans transitioned from a nomadic lifestyle to settled farming communities. This gradual shift allowed them to cultivate crops and domesticate animals, eliminating the need for constant movement in search of resources. Permanent settlements emerged, leading to the development of more complex work structures.[5]

Despite the shift to settled agriculture, work remained predominantly manual and physically demanding. However, the introduction of currency and trade brought new possibilities, gradually enabling the growth of specialized crafts and services. Skilled artisans emerged, honing their expertise in areas such as metalwork and tool manufacturing. Early examples of structured work organizations can be seen in armies and monasteries, which pioneered integrated management and production systems.[6]

During medieval times, the rise of cities introduced a new phenomenon: craftsmanship. Young men became apprentices, learning their crafts from skilled masters in workshops, such as painters or silversmiths. Work took on a sense of mission and purpose, often intertwined with religious beliefs. Guilds formed, organizing and shaping the craft industry and, in some cases, wielding political power that influenced society.[7]

The Renaissance period of the fourteenth and fifteenth centuries witnessed a flourishing of the arts and the emergence of new forms of work. Scientific advances and discoveries laid the foundations for commerce, trade, legal systems, and finance. While the majority of people still engaged in manual labor, a small minority pursued non-manual work, including royalty, early scientists, religious institutions, and the military. However, the scale of non-manual labor remained relatively small compared to agricultural work.

Work during this era started to develop basic structures and mechanisms to support growing populations, towns, and armies. Although still rudimentary, it laid the groundwork for the future evolution of work. We can refer to this phase as Work 1.0, the first mature version of work.

As we examine the historical progress of work, we gain a deeper understanding of its origins and how it has evolved over time. The transition from survival-driven work to specialized crafts and emerging systems sets the stage for the transformations that lie ahead. Join me as we continue our journey through the history of work, exploring how subsequent developments have shaped the modern work landscape and paving the way for the challenges and opportunities of the present day.

Notes

1. Gallup (2022). The state of the global workplace. Gallup, Inc. https://www.gallup.com/workplace/393395/world-workplace-broken-fix.aspx
2. Robert Tressell, *The Ragged-Trousered Philanthropists* (London: Lawrence & Wishart, 1955).
3. *Oxford English Dictionary*, Work. www.oxfordlearnersdictionaries.com
4. John Brass, *Work and the Beast: An Essay in Cultural Evolution* (New York: Harper & Row, 1975.) Richard B. Lee, *Man the Hunter* (New York: Oxford University Press, 1968).
5. Colin Renfrew, *The Neolithic Revolution: The Rise of Agriculture and Civilization* (London: Jonathan Cape, 1972).
6. N. Nicholson, The design of work: An evolutionary perspective. *Journal of Organizational Behavior*, 31 (2010): 422–431.
7. Louis Dupré, *Work: The Gift of Meaning and Dignity* (New York: Crossroad, 1996).

CHAPTER 3
THE INDUSTRIAL REVOLUTION: HELLO, WORK 2.0

Work 2.0: The impact of the industrial revolution

With the arrival of the industrial revolution, work underwent a profound transformation. The invention of machines capable of performing tasks previously done by many individuals resulted in the rise of factories and the rapid growth of urban areas. Work became more basic, requiring hard skills, and physical in nature, with individuals focusing on jobs that aligned with their skills.

The organization of work underwent three significant cycles that fundamentally changed how the economy generated value. These cycles can be categorized as: (1) pre-industrial; (2) industrial; and (3) post-industrial, with our current era being in the post-industrial cycle.

Before the industrial revolution in the 1800s, the majority of work was done by hand, as most people were either farmers or craftsmen. Division of labor was minimal, and individuals were responsible for performing a wide range of tasks themselves. Exceptions existed for larger organizations such as the military, trading businesses, construction companies, and agricultural enterprises. Human and animal energy, occasionally supplemented by water wheels, powered these workspaces.

During the pre-industrial era, there was little to no formal management. Owners themselves handled tasks, such as coordination, rewards, and resource allocation. People were employed for their entire lives, and concepts like "career switching" or "work-life balance" did not exist because work was not a choice—it was a means of survival. The purpose of work was solely to sustain life.

However, glimpses of change emerged through the thoughts of thinkers like Adam Smith, who recognized that the division of labor and specialization could enhance productivity. The arrival of the industrial revolution brought about a revolutionary leap in work. It marked the first golden age of innovation, as tremendous transformations occurred in a relatively short period.

The dawn of the industrial revolution occurred in the mid-eighteenth century, predominantly in the North of England. This period marked a major turning point in human history as a flurry of technological advances completely overturned the conventional work landscape. This transition period, often referred to as the First Industrial Revolution, spanned roughly from the 1760s to the 1840s.

The revolution was initiated by the advent of mechanized textile production, with the proliferation of mills predominantly dedicated to cotton production. These factories offered employment opportunities to farm workers, drawing them into urban areas and leading to a significant shift in workforce demographics. Thus, the period was marked by the population migration from rural to urban areas, and the consequent emergence of factory towns.

While the initial phase of the industrial revolution was primarily dominated by textile production and coal mining, the subsequent years witnessed progressive advances in technology. These included new methods of steelmaking, the development of product assembly lines for mass production, the invention of large-scale machine tools, and the creation of electrical grids. The invention of steam-powered machinery was a transformative addition, signifying a key transition from manual labor to mechanized work.

We can be grateful that we do not work under the conditions faced by workers in the industrial revolution. To say that the work was brutal would be an understatement. Factory employees were treated badly, paid meager wages, and the work itself was monotonous and unfulfilling. Factory jobs were seen as last resorts, and individuals took them because they had no other options.

There were no age restrictions for work, and individuals started working in factories at a young age—sometimes as early as 10 or 11 years old. They endured long working hours, often for the entire day.

Life expectancy during the industrial revolution was tragically short, typically lasting only until a person's mid-20s. Poor working conditions and a lack of safety regulations contributed to this. Most factory workers did not earn enough to support themselves and their families.

As the industrial revolution unfolded, a new way of organizing work had to be invented to support the factory system. The management practices we know today were born on the factory floor, driven by the need to maximize output. Productivity and quality were measured, and each machine required an operator to produce the desired output.

By the end of the nineteenth century, approximately 20% of people in Europe and the United States were employed in manufacturing. However, agriculture remained the primary source of work, with the majority of the population engaged in farming and related activities. Services, mining, and domestic work accounted for the remaining jobs.

The foundations of knowledge work were laid during this period, thanks to inventions like the steam engine, electricity, the telephone, the light bulb, and the sewing machine. However, knowledge work remained relatively nascent, and only a small proportion of the global population was engaged in these pursuits.

Work 2.0 emerged as a result of the industrial revolution, leading to a division of labor and specialization. This transformation was closely tied to the increasing sophistication of machines and factories. From producing textiles in the early 1800s, factories expanded to manufacture engines, light bulbs, machinery, and infrastructure by the end of the nineteenth century.

During this time, the concept of "time equals money" took hold. Factory workers were often paid by the hour, directly linking time to their earnings. The notion that working hard and long hours equated to success became deeply ingrained. It blended in well with the American dream, as industries and infrastructure were built from the ground up through the tireless efforts of individuals.

While the early stages of the industrial revolution resulted in a net increase in employment, as more workers were needed to operate machines in factories and construct infrastructure, technological advances and improved efficiency eventually led to unemployment and underemployment. The growth in population followed, driven in part by the use of machines in farming, which increased food production capacity and sparked an economic boom.

In summary, the industrial revolution served as a major global catalyst for transforming work, reshaping the way people lived, worked, and interacted with one another. Urbanization, the rise of factories, and the emergence of a working class were among the significant changes that occurred. As we move forward, we'll explore the subsequent waves of change in work and their impact on society, leading us to the present-day work landscape.

Lifetime employment

Let's fast forward 100 years and two world wars later to the year 1956 in Japan. We meet Mr. Tanaka, who had joined a Japanese company as a young man five years earlier. He worked diligently and cherished the stability and security provided by the company. During this time, lifetime employment was common in Japan as companies experienced rapid growth and competed for talented workers.

As Mr. Tanaka advanced in age, he climbed the corporate ladder and eventually became a manager. He took pride in his contributions to the company and felt a deep sense of loyalty toward his employer. However, as the Japanese economy changed and the company faced challenges, Mr. Tanaka found himself at a crossroads. The company underwent restructuring and could no longer guarantee lifetime employment. This put Mr. Tanaka in a difficult position, as he had devoted his entire career to the company and was unsure of what he would do without it. In the end, he chose to retire early.

The concept of lifetime employment originated in post-World War II Japan. It was implemented as a means to ensure stability and loyalty in the workforce during a period of high economic growth. Companies offered job security in exchange for employee commitment and hard work.

While lifetime employment found its place in various parts of the world, including Japan, Korea, the United States, and Europe, many businesses eventually had to let go of this practice. They realized that it hindered the flexibility necessary in a dynamic economy and it had become a strategic burden. Consequently, companies had to break promises made to their employees and abandon lifetime employment arrangements.

Drawing parallels with marriage is apt, as there was often an extensive courting or dating process before a mutual lifetime commitment was made. Companies evaluated potential employees, and individuals also assessed the company's fit for their long-term goals.

Although lifetime employment is not prevalent in most parts of the world today, Asian countries such as Japan and South Korea still maintain significant practices of lifetime employment in certain niche industries. I had the opportunity to spend time with senior human resources executives and junior staff members who worked under lifetime employment arrangements in Japan and Korea. It felt like stepping back into the past. Undoubtedly, the stability of working for a single company was valued within their families and seen as a success. However, individuals in these roles were not necessarily thrilled with the lack of choice and freedom that came with it.

Typically, recruitment for lifetime employment occurs right after university, with rigorous entry tests to assess long-term fit with organizations. Once hired, new employees are placed in their first role with limited or no input from the individuals. Lack of choice was a hallmark of lifetime employment. While you were a necessary part of the corporation, you had to leave your personal freedom and ability to choose at the door.

We will delve deeper into the intricacies of lifetime employment later on, but it's important to acknowledge that not everything is perfect in the universe of lifetime employment.

Total Quality Management (TQM)

Now, let's turn our focus to the culmination of the factory management approach, which took nearly a century to refine and was formalized by one of Japan's most renowned companies: Toyota. Toyota's application of Total Quality Management (TQM)[1] in manufacturing internal combustion cars, considered the pinnacle of the industrial revolution, exemplified a complex system comprising over 2,000 parts that required separate manufacturing, assembly, and meticulous quality control. These cars were mass-produced and bought by millions of people worldwide.

TQM, a framework that continuously optimized the factory system to achieve the highest level of quality while maintaining large-scale output, enabled Toyota to achieve unparalleled efficiency, quality, and productivity. This approach set the gold standard for work management in factories globally.

TQM is built upon six fundamental pillars. The first pillar places the customer at the center of all decision-making, prioritizing their needs and expectations. TQM encourages constant evaluation and improvement across all aspects of the business, from production processes to employee training. Data-driven processes guide decision-making, enhancing efficiency and effectiveness. TQM fosters a collaborative and inclusive work environment where employees work together to achieve common goals. Finally, TQM emphasizes strong leadership that provides clear direction, sets high standards, and establishes a culture of quality.

By integrating these principles into daily operations, the TQM approach allowed Toyota to become a benchmark for factory productivity. As the largest auto-manufacturer globally, producing 9.2 million cars in 2022, Toyota is renowned for its uncompromising approach to quality and reliability. However, the focus on incremental optimization and maximizing productivity and quality can inadvertently limit creativity. When people are aware that experimentation or new approaches may disrupt the efficiency of factory processes, they become less likely to explore innovative ideas.

This approach may be ideal when developing a craft in a stable and predictable environment. It's not surprising that it emerged in Japan, a country with a long history of mastering crafts.

Six Sigma

In parallel with developments in Japan, in the mid-1980s, Motorola, facing challenges in high-end precision manufacturing, developed the Six Sigma[2] work methodology. The company sought a new approach to improve processes and reduce defects as competition increased and quality issues arose.

Engineers and quality experts at Motorola, including Bill Smith and Mikel Harry, crafted Six Sigma as a structured and data-driven approach to continuous improvement. The goal of Six Sigma was to reduce defects to a rate of 3.4 per million opportunities, representing six standard deviations from the mean.

Six Sigma became a widely adopted, data-driven, and continuous improvement methodology that provides companies with the tools to reduce defects and increase efficiency in business processes. The Six Sigma methodology follows five steps: Define, Measure, Analyze, Improve, and Control (DMAIC). These steps involve defining the problem, measuring performance, analyzing data to identify root causes, implementing solutions to improve performance, and controlling the process to ensure sustained improvement.

Six Sigma found its place as the second pinnacle of factory productivity through its adoption by General Electric (GE).

In the 1990s, GE was one of the largest and most diversified conglomerates globally, operating in various industries, including aviation, power generation, consumer appliances, and financial services. GE was renowned for its strong brand, financial stability, and innovation, led by the legendary CEO Jack Welch, widely regarded as a visionary and one of the best CEOs in business history.

GE employed several different work methodologies, with Six Sigma being one of the most prominent. The company utilized Six Sigma to drive improvements across multiple areas, including operations, engineering, and customer service.

Summary

The concept of work has evolved significantly from the preindustrial age to the present post-industrial era. The industrial revolution brought forth Work 2.0, characterized by the rise of factories, specialization, and division of labor, driven by the relentless pursuit of efficiency and quality. Pivotal practices and methodologies such as lifetime employment, Total Quality Management, and Six Sigma emerged during this transformative period.

Notes

1. TQM. https://www.toyota-global.com/company/history_of_toyota/75years/data/company_information/management_and_finances/management/tqm/change.html
2. Six Sigma. https://sixsigmadsi.com/a-brief-history-of-six-sigma/

CHAPTER 4
WORK 2.5 AND GETTING STUCK

The post-industrial revolution

The first 150 years of the work revolution augmented and replaced many forms of manual labor, allowing our time, focus, and energy to be applied elsewhere. However, the last 50 years have focused on augmenting intellectual and knowledge capabilities. This was achieved through the accumulation of knowledge in universally accessible locations and increased computing power and connectivity. The upcoming phase will involve automating low-intelligence activities, challenging the value that many people bring to work and fundamentally reshaping work.

During the post-industrial revolution, competition for talent intensified due to increased productivity and economic growth. More jobs were available than there were people to fill them. This led to the concept of paying for skills, which essentially meant being paid for time with an expectation that time equals output. While this link may have been clear when people worked on machines in factories, establishing the same link for service and problem-solving jobs became more challenging.

The invention of computers and the internet in the late 1980s brought about further changes in the nature of work. Work shifted into the realm of knowledge work, with manufacturing and traditional factory work accounting for a smaller percentage compared to services, trade, and the knowledge economy. Old jobs disappeared while new ones emerged. Work was no longer limited to a physical place; it could now be done from anywhere in the world.

The form of work we know today is a by-product of industrialized work with digitalization added on top. However, work has significantly changed since then, and three major shifts have fundamentally transformed it:

- **Globalization:** Work is no longer limited to a single place and can span continents. The internet and upcoming global satellite networks, like Starlink, will provide connectivity to every corner of the world, allowing work to be done from anywhere.

- **Transition from specialists to generalists:** We are shifting from work done by people who specialize in specific skills to generalists with broad knowledge and the ability to solve complex problems through pattern matching and creative solutions.

- **Standardization and commoditization:** During the industrial revolution, work became standardized and commoditized. A pair of hands was needed to complement machines and ensure their continuous operation. The focus shifted from craftsmen producing custom, handmade goods to mass production and increased output.

The factory mindset of work continues to cast a long shadow over the way we think about management today. This mindset assumes that stability is the norm and change is the exception. However, we now live in a post-industrial age where the efficiency of manufacturing has reached a high level, and the majority of people are employed in services and the knowledge economy. The factory mindset no longer serves us well for the complexity and mental effort required in today's kind of work. Simply having someone at their desk for 10 hours is insufficient to solve complex problems; the new work requires deep engagement, creativity, and concentration.

In the past, engagement and enjoyment were not associated with work. People punched in and out, and time, strength, and skill were the currency of the industrial revolution. However, this factory-oriented mindset is ill-suited for knowledge work.

In the industrial revolution, work was primarily measured by the amount of work done in a specific time period. Tangible outputs, such as the number of products manufactured, determined work productivity. This type of work was highly structured and required little autonomy from workers.

Today, work is different. It is measured by the quality of output and creative thinking rather than tangible outputs. This type of work demands engagement from employees, involving complex problem-solving, decision-making, and the ability to work independently or collaboratively.

We have been sold a false happiness story, one that equates more money with more things and more free time for relaxation. This story served its purpose to mobilize large parts of the population to join the workforce and fuel the consumer economy. However, work remains a necessity for living, and society has traditionally required everyone to work for economic output, competitiveness, and long-term viability.

As modern life progresses, we are transitioning to a phase where computers take on tasks that were once limited to human capabilities. We are breaking through the barrier of one person, one brain. It is foreseeable that society and countries will no longer need to maximize the absolute output from each member by making them work for a living. Work is undergoing a revolution, and many organizations have not shifted their approach from the industrial revolution model to something more suitable for the twenty-first century. This mismatch between employee expectations and organizational practices leads to dissatisfaction and disengagement in the workplace.

Work should be more like a game, designed to engage, motivate, and make us feel good. We need to create work environments where we can thrive. The way work is currently structured largely resembles the industrial revolution model, which focused on efficiency and output. However, this approach is no longer effective in our modern world, and it fails to make us truly happy.

New ways of working

In recent years, various innovative models of work have emerged, such as outsourcing, the gig economy, freelancing, and alternative work arrangements like the four-day workweek and working from home. These models have challenged traditional notions of work and offer alternative ways of organizing and performing tasks.

So, are we stuck in outdated work structures, and what can we do about it? The answer lies in front of us, and we will explore it further in Chapter 5. Before diving into the reasons behind our current state of being stuck in the factory-like work loop, let's take a look at some recent innovative models of work.

Outsourcing

Outsourcing, which originated in the United States in the 1960s, involves companies contracting with external entities or individuals to perform tasks, services, or functions previously handled by their own employees. This typically includes tasks like manufacturing, customer service, and IT support. The main goal of outsourcing is usually to reduce costs and improve efficiency by leveraging lower labor costs or specialized expertise offered by external providers.

Initially, outsourcing focused on low-skilled or manual tasks, such as manufacturing or data entry. However, advances in technology and increased globalization have expanded outsourcing to encompass a broader range of activities, including high-skilled tasks like software development, engineering, and financial analysis.

Currently, outsourcing employs an estimated 14.3 million people in the United States alone, with significant levels of outsourcing to countries such as India, the Philippines, and China.

The gig economy

The gig economy emerged in the late 2000s in the United States and has since become a global phenomenon. It refers to jobs characterized by short-term work or freelancing, rather than traditional permanent employment.

Work in the gig economy is often organized around individual tasks or projects, offering workers flexibility in choosing when and where they work. However, gig workers often lack the stability and benefits associated with traditional employment, such as health insurance, pensions, or paid time off.

Digital platforms play a central role in connecting gig workers with customers, acting as intermediaries and facilitating payment and support. The rise of the internet has opened up new opportunities for people to earn money and engage in work on their terms.

Initially, most gig economy work focused on simple, low-skilled tasks like goods and food delivery, ride-sharing, cleaning, and packaging. These tasks were easier to match with available demand and supply.

Freelancing

Freelancing, which overlaps with gigs, typically involves skilled work performed by individuals who are not directly employed by companies on a full-time basis. Freelancers work on a project-by-project basis and are self-employed, often working from home or remotely, using their own tools and equipment. They are compensated for the services they provide, whether by the hour, day, or project.

In 2020, there were an estimated 57 million freelancers in the United States, representing approximately 36% of the workforce.[1] Similarly, in Europe, the number of freelancers is estimated to have increased by 40% between 2013 and 2018.[2] The rise of freelancing is driven by technological advances and changes in the nature of work.

Four-day workweek

As early as 1960, the concept of a shorter four-day workweek gained popularity as a means to improve the work-life balance and reduce commuting time. In a four-day workweek, employees work the same number of total hours, but those hours are spread out over four days instead of five.

The idea has been further popularized in recent years as a way for companies to increase productivity, reduce burnout, and boost employee morale. Many organizations have tested and implemented the four-day workweek, especially in response to the COVID-19 pandemic, which has sparked increased interest in alternative work arrangements.

However, some argue that a four-day workweek may decrease overall productivity while maintaining similar labor costs.

Working from home

The concept of working from home, also known as telecommuting, has been around since the 1970s. It gained popularity in the 1990s with the widespread adoption of personal computers and the internet. Working from home aimed to improve the work-life balance and reduce commuting traffic.

Initially, only a small minority of companies allowed remote work. However, the COVID-19 pandemic forced a global transition to working from home, making it the norm for the majority of the world's workforce of 3.2 billion people.

Contrary to concerns about decreased productivity, many employees reported being more productive while working from home. Additionally, remote work has allowed for a better balance between work and personal life, eliminated commuting time and expenses, and reduced office space costs for employers. However, it has also brought challenges related to control, collaboration, innovation, and mental health.

The shift toward working from home has also begun to reshape our urban economies and communities. It has far-reaching implications for people working in ancillary industries that once thrived on supporting the daily commuting workforce. Those who work in city center cafes, pubs, and restaurants that used to buzz with lunchtime traffic from nearby offices, now find their places quieter with only a few customers dropping by. Likewise, bus and train drivers who brought workers to and from offices now navigate emptier routes, with their own employment at risk.

As we conclude this exploration of the history of work, it becomes evident that the current work structures do not align well with the new reality of work. In Chapter 5, we will dive deeper into the causes of our state of being stuck and discover ways to break free from outdated models.

Notes

1. Upwork. (2020). The state of freelancing in America. https://www.upwork.com/i/freelancing-in-america/
2. Eurostat. (2019). European Union Labour Force Survey (EU LFS) 2018 results. https://ec.europa.eu/eurostat/web/microdata/european-union-labour-force-survey

CHAPTER 5
WORK 3.0: THE INTERNET WORK REVOLUTION

Reflecting on the fast-paced changes that characterize Work 3.0, the fundamental shifts in the economy, the global generational shifts, and the fact that the majority of working adults have been indoctrinated into the old proven industrial work approach, we begin to comprehend why we're feeling stuck. The gap between our Work 2.0 strategies and the challenges of Work 3.0 has widened too quickly and to bridge it we need to transform our understanding of work.

This transformation starts with re-evaluating the evolving, human-centric problems of Work 3.0 and blending this with the latest insights from neuroscience that reveal why we are drawn to specific challenging activities. By identifying the hard tasks that we naturally find enjoyable, we can forge a connection between our true motivators and future job demands. This newfound self-awareness can guide us to redesign human-centric work, paving the way toward a career that better harmonizes with our core interests and enhances our work happiness.

The rise of the internet economy has ushered in a new era of work, often referred to as Work 3.0. This era is characterized by the transformative power of the internet and its impact on employment and business models.

The internet economy now constitutes nearly 20% of the global economy and associated GDP,[1] a remarkable achievement considering its relatively short existence of just over 20 years. The internet has fundamentally transformed economies worldwide.

One significant effect of the internet economy is the automation of routine tasks, leading to a reduced reliance on human labor in certain industries. Simultaneously, it has opened up new job opportunities in fields like software development, data analytics, and digital marketing.

Moreover, the internet economy has disrupted traditional business models, giving rise to new companies and industries that were previously unimaginable. This has intensified competition and necessitated adaptation and change for established businesses.

AI coming after our work

At the time of writing, a new wave of Artificial Intelligence (AI) is attracting attention and sparking debates and concerns regarding the future of work. Platforms like ChatGPT, developed by OpenAI, have garnered immense popularity within months of their release. ChatGPT alone has reached 100 million monthly active users, making it the fastest-growing platform ever. Surprisingly, AI models like ChatGPT have demonstrated the ability to pass university exams, including specialized fields like MBA and Legal Bar Exams, using the knowledge accumulated from the internet.

The current wave of AI, known as language models, has been trained on a vast range of internet text comprising websites, books, and social media platforms. This training process requires several months on state-of-the-art hardware, including high-end microprocessors.

AI language models utilize machine learning techniques to predict the next word in a sequence of text, based on the preceding context. They learn patterns and relationships between words and phrases in the language by processing extensive amounts of text data.

Neural networks, inspired by the structure and function of the human brain, are the most common type of AI language models. These models adjust their parameters during training to minimize the difference between their predictions and the actual text.

AI language models find applications in text generation, classification, machine translation, sentiment analysis, and more. The quality and capabilities of language models have significantly improved in recent years, leading to their adoption across various industries and fields.

The implications of AI language models extend beyond basic calculations; they have the potential to automate or assist with tasks involving simpler intelligence work. For example, they can help with legal research, finding relevant precedents, or analyzing information from various sources to draw strategic implications.

We stand on the brink of another significant inflection point in the world of work. When asked about the types of work that AI is likely to automate or replace, ChatGPT responds in a non-threatening manner, providing a glimpse into what lies ahead.

It's important to note that AI language models are not intended to replace human workers entirely. Instead, they aim to support and streamline certain tasks, freeing up time and resources for more complex and creative endeavors that require human judgment and expertise.

Some tasks that AI language models are likely to replace or augment include data entry and transcription, content generation, text summarization, and customer service. Additionally, AI language models have the potential to serve as personal assistant coaches, helping individuals navigate through the influx of emails, reports, and messages, filtering out irrelevant information and highlighting actionable insights that truly require attention.

Generation XYZ

As we delve into the topic of generational differences, it becomes apparent that every generation has its unique traits and perspectives. Engaging in conversations with older individuals, you'll often hear them claim to be harder-working and more serious, while younger generations argue that the older folks are stuck in their old ways, working inefficiently.

The interplay between nature and nurture plays a significant role in shaping generational cohorts. Shared experiences of major events, cultural shifts, economic cycles, and technological leaps create a common generational substrate. These experiences not only influence how individuals think about these events but also shape the narratives created by each generation.

Within the context of work, different generations approach work in different ways. While certain fundamental truths remain constant, influenced by our biological hardware, the software of our brains is influenced by societal norms, generational interpretations, and country-specific histories. Intrinsic motivations tend to stay the same across generations, while subtle differences may arise in the interpretation of what constitutes extrinsic motivation.

For instance, in Asian societies, there is often a stronger societal and community focus on financial achievements, leading to the prominence of extrinsic motivations. However, this does not necessarily mean that individuals will choose games or pursuits solely based on achievement. It may result in someone opting for a competitive esports career not solely out of passion for the game but because it offers the highest financial returns.

Another dimension of intergenerational differences in work lies in the younger generation's adaptability and openness to new approaches. Take Generation Z, for example, the cohort entering the workforce now. They value flexibility, a good work-life balance, personal and professional development, practical learning, innovation, and creativity.

In contrast, Generation X is often described as independent, resourceful, and adaptable. They prioritize a good work-life balance, flexibility, personal development, and possess a problem-solving attitude. They value stability, efficiency, and results-oriented work environments, while also excelling in communication, leadership, and teamwork.

Meanwhile, millennials are often characterized as tech-savvy, confident, and optimistic. They prioritize diversity, inclusivity, a good work-life balance, flexible schedules, and opportunities for growth. Collaboration, transparency, and open communication are essential to them, and they approach work with a sense of purpose and a desire for meaningful work. They are comfortable with technology and expect it to play a significant role in their professional lives.

During my conversation with the CEO of a leading human resources provider and temporary staffing firm, she acknowledged the rapidly changing nature of work. She agreed that the notion of employees staying with a company for 10 years, once the norm, is now outdated. With a significant proportion of her team in their mid-20s, she revealed that the average tenure in their company is 18 months and that is rapidly dropping. She predicted an increase in staff turnover in the foreseeable future.

Intriguingly, she shared that her company is already transitioning to a 2-day in-office setup with no Friday meetings. When I questioned the level of autonomy this arrangement truly provided, she admitted that while these steps were in the right direction, they were not the ultimate destination.

Another fascinating initiative she mentioned was the introduction of a top performer award, where the winner receives an honor in the form of a fancy gaming chair for the month. This not only enhanced sitting comfort but also served as a form of peer signaling. She stated that this approach had yielded remarkable results, igniting noticeable excitement within her team of nearly 200 employees. There was an ongoing competition among them to win these coveted chairs. This approach, not unlike the traditional employee of the month award, appeared to resonate with a specific group of individuals—those driven by extrinsic motivation and achievement. She acknowledged that the majority of people they attracted to their team were motivated by commission-based compensation, making this initiative a natural fit.

As I concluded my conversation with the CEO, it became clear that work is evolving at a rapid pace. Her company's adoption of a 2-day office setup, the implementation of exciting incentives, and the recognition that change is inevitable made them a pioneering organization, ahead of the pack and a potential bellwether of what lies ahead.

The future of work is being shaped by the values, preferences, and adaptability of different generations, each with its unique perspectives and aspirations. Embracing these differences and creating work environments that cater to the evolving needs of employees are essential for organizations to thrive in the Work 3.0 era.

Summary

Chapter 5 began by explaining the gap between our Work 2.0 strategies and the challenges of Work 3.0 has widened too quickly, and to bridge it, and so we need to transform our understanding of work, to get out of our state of being stuck.

The chapter then explores the transformative impact of both the internet economy and AI language models on the way we work. The internet economy has revolutionized industries, automated routine tasks, and created new job opportunities in fields like software development and digital marketing. It has also disrupted traditional business models, leading to increased competition and the need for adaptation.

The emergence of AI language models, such as ChatGPT, has sparked debates about intelligence and work. These models, trained on vast amounts of text data, can generate sophisticated language and pass exams previously reserved for humans. They have the potential to automate or augment various tasks in industries that involve processing and generating text data.

The chapter also dives into the concept of generational differences in work. Each generation brings its unique perspectives and approaches to work, shaped by shared experiences and societal factors. Understanding and accommodating these differences can lead to more effective and harmonious work environments.

Furthermore, the CEO of a leading HR provider shared insights on the changing nature of work. With an average tenure of 18 months and a shift toward a freelance workforce, organizations are adapting to the evolving expectations and preferences of younger generations. Initiatives like flexible work arrangements and incentive programs tailored to individual motivations are becoming more prevalent.

The chapter concludes by emphasizing the need to reimagine work in the context of Work 3.0. Striking a balance between automation and human expertise, fostering flexibility and adaptability, and prioritizing personal growth and well-being are crucial for navigating the future of work successfully.

As we move forward, the traditional norms and structures of work must be reassessed to create environments that support productivity, innovation, and fulfillment for individuals across generations. The future of work lies in leveraging technology, understanding generational dynamics, and embracing the changing nature of work to shape a more inclusive, flexible, and purpose-driven work ecosystem.

Note

1. United Nations Conference on Trade and Development (UNCTAD). (2019). Digital Economy Report 2019: Overview. https://unctad.org/system/files/official-document/der2019_overview_en.pdf. doi:10.18356/88774

PART II
WHO SAID IT CAN'T BE ALL FUN AND GAMES?

CHAPTER 6
DESIGNING FUN:
THE MAGIC OF GAMES

The game invokes an experience in players' mind.

—Jesse Schell[1]

In every job that must be done
There is an element of fun.
You find the fun and snap!
The job's a game.

—[A spoonful of sugar] *Mary Poppins*

When I engage in video games, I feel an exhilarating sense of aliveness. As I pick up a controller or turn on my PC, the mundane world fades away, and a captivating realm comes to life. In this realm, I can be anyone or anything I desire, simply by choosing the right game. Sometimes, I gather my friends online, and we play for hours on end, completely absorbed in the experience. Time slips away, and it's only when I glance at the clock and realize it's 2 AM that I reluctantly decided to get some sleep before another day of work begins. Games hold a special place in my heart.

Games are truly unique, offering an experience unlike any other. They differ from riding roller coasters, petting animals, or even watching movies. But have you ever tried describing fun to a 5-year-old without using the word "fun"? It's quite a challenge, isn't it? Fun is subjective, as it can be experienced in various ways—playing games with friends, dancing with strangers, or sharing laughter with family. So, what exactly constitutes true fun?

In her book, *The Power of Fun*,[2] Catherine Price defines fun as "an activity that produces a state of mind characterized by high levels of pleasure, engagement, and a sense of personal fulfillment." Fun is a subjective experience that varies from person to person, encompassing a wide range of activities, from hobbies and sports to socializing and creative pursuits. Prioritizing fun in our lives is vital, as it can improve our mental and emotional well-being, enhance our motivation and creativity, and strengthen our relationships with others.

Fun is an enjoyable and entertaining activity that brings us pleasure, excitement, and happiness. It takes many forms, from engaging in physical activities and playing games to trying new things or simply spending time with loved ones. Fun provides a refreshing break from our everyday routines, infusing light-heartedness and joy into our lives. It is an essential element for a well-rounded existence, reducing stress, fostering positivity, and promoting overall well-being.

So, what sets games apart from other experiences? Games create a unique and immersive journey in our minds. Unlike books, where we absorb symbols on a page and imagine the rest, games involve active participation, allowing us not only to experience the story but also to shape it.

Let's explore five essential components that lie at the heart of what makes a game a game, namely rules, goals, obstacles, agency, and feedback:

- **Rules:** Every game has a set of rules that govern how it is played and how players interact with each other and the game world. Some rules are explicitly stated, while others are discovered through experimentation and exploration.

- **Goals:** Games have objectives or goals that players strive to achieve. These can include winning over opponents, solving puzzles, or reaching specific levels of progress. Goals provide direction and purpose within the game.

- **Obstacles:** Games present players with challenges and obstacles that must be overcome to achieve the goals. The best games strike a balance between difficulty and achievability, allowing players to enter a state of flow[3]—a sweet spot where challenges align with their capabilities.

- **Agency:** Games empower players with agency—the ability to influence and shape the course of events within the game. Unlike passive forms of media, games give players control over their actions and decisions, making their experience deeply engaging and personal.

- **Feedback:** Finally, games provide quick and tangible feedback to players, typically in the form of scores, points, or indicators of progress. This feedback reinforces a sense of achievement, allowing players to track their success and adjust their strategies accordingly.

Interestingly, we are not compelled to play games unless we choose to do so. With the exception of game testers and esports professionals, most of us engage in games purely of our own free will. We have the autonomy to select the games we want to play and decide how long we want to play them. If a game fails to capture our interest, we are free to move on. It's this freedom of choice that adds to the appeal and enjoyment of games.

A player's experience of a game is a complex interplay of cognitive and emotional processes. As players immerse themselves in the game environment, their senses absorb information—visuals, sounds, and gameplay mechanics. Their minds construct a mental model of the game world, which they use to make decisions and navigate the game. Emotions and motivations play a crucial role, too, as players feel excitement, frustration, satisfaction, and other emotions while playing. These emotions influence their enjoyment of the game and their willingness to continue playing.

Games have been an integral part of human history, dating back to ancient times. They are embedded in all cultures and represent one of the oldest forms of social interaction.

Some claim that Senet, an ancient Egyptian board game, is the oldest known game. It involved moving pieces along a board, aiming to reach the end and attain the afterlife. The game's rules are not entirely known, but its popularity in ancient Egypt is evident from its depiction in tombs and artifacts of the period.

Games have come a long way in the past 5,470 years, usually involving interaction between two or more people. Lately people have been playing games with a computer instead of another person.

At this point, let's differentiate between games, puzzles, and toys. Puzzles are problem-solving activities with a single solution, often created by puzzle makers. Once solved, puzzles tend to lose their appeal. Toys, on the other hand, are playthings designed for entertainment, lacking explicit objectives or built-in problems. They offer room for imagination but lack a defined purpose.

Games, however, possess a unique power—the power of wish fulfillment. When we engage with games, we find ourselves fully immersed, experiencing a sense of agency and adventure. Especially once we jump from traditional board games into the vibrant universe of video games. Video games invite us to step into extraordinary worlds and embark on remarkable journeys, where we are not mere spectators but active participants, shaping our own destinies within the game. Video games harness the power of technology to turbo-charge game-play to new levels and give us a perfectly matched digital opponent.

In Chapter 7, we will explore the diverse genres and types of games, discovering the vast landscapes that await us as players and creators alike. Together, we will unlock the secrets of game design and discover how to create experiences that captivate, inspire, and ignite the spark of fun within every player.

Notes

1. Jesse Schell, *The Art of Game Design: A Book of Lenses* (Boca Raton. FL: CRC Press, 2008).
2. Catherine Price. *The Power of Fun* (New York: Bantam Press, 2022).
3. The concept of flow, pioneered by psychologist Mihaly Csikszentmihalyi in his seminal work, posits that individuals experience optimal satisfaction and productivity when their skill level appropriately matches the challenge at hand. In a state of flow, people lose their sense of time and self, becoming completely absorbed in the task, or the game, in our case.

CHAPTER 7
GAMES GIVE US A RAY OF HOPE

Games can unlock our inner motivations – beyond extrinsic rewards like money or status – by tapping into intrinsic sources of joy such as curiosity, problem-solving, and creativity.
—Adam Grant, author of *Originals*

I have a confession to make: I'm a big fan of video games. In fact, it was my love for games that led me to pursue a career in software engineering when I was a younger. I had a simple desire—to make money so I could buy a better computer to play even better video games. It wasn't about saving the world; it was about the joy of gaming. Elon Musk, CEO of Tesla and Space X, shares a similar sentiment, emphasizing how video games sparked his passion for technology and innovation.

Fortunately, the landscape of work is not as bleak as it may seem. There is a way to make it better, and I hinted at it in the beginning of this book—it's games. So, let's delve into why games are the ultimate tool and why we play them in the first place.

First and foremost, we will define what games are. Interestingly, there isn't a universally agreed-upon definition, as the term encompasses a wide range of activities. While it's enlightening to examine the simplest of games to understand their fundamental elements, we are particularly interested in games with more complexity and longevity.

Games come in various forms: board games, card games, sports games, playground games, party games, gambling, puzzles, arcade games, electronic games, computer games, and video games. To grasp the essence of games, let's turn to Jesse Schell's defining book on game design, *The Art of Game Design*,[1] which has stood the test of time.

According to Schell, "Play is manipulation that indulges curiosity." It's about satisfying our personal curiosity and exploring the answers to our burning questions, rather than simply earning money to pay the bills. Games are an exercise of voluntary control systems, where powers are pitted against each other within the confines of rules, aiming to produce an unbalanced outcome. Elliot Avedon and Brian Sutton-Smith[2] further describe games as voluntary problem-solving activities.

Schell raises an intriguing point about gambling games, which may appear to be an exception at first. Is someone playing cards truly trying to solve a problem? He affirms that they are. The problem they seek to solve revolves around taking calculated risks and maximizing financial gains.

This insight supports the notion that problem-solving is not only attractive to us but also an integral part of what makes games fun. Isn't that fascinating?

Now, let's address puzzles. Are they truly games, or do they belong to a different category altogether? At times, while sitting in front of a 1,000-piece puzzle, I find myself pondering this question. It turns out that puzzles do contain elements of games, but they are rather one-directional—a game with a predetermined path to a solution. Once we solve a puzzle, we rarely feel compelled to solve it again.

Thus, we agree that games are activities characterized by structured rules, challenges, and competition or cooperation among participants. They can be played for entertainment, recreation, or competition, and they come in many different forms, such as physical games, board games, card games, video games, and more.

To distill it further, games involve a few common characteristics, in addition to the goals and rules that we identified:

- **Competition or cooperation:** Games involve competition or cooperation among players. In competitive games, players may compete against each other directly, such as in a game of soccer, or they may compete to achieve a shared goal, such as in a cooperative board game. Cooperative games entail players working together to accomplish a common objective, as seen in team-based video games.

- **Randomness or uncertainty:** Many games incorporate an element of randomness or uncertainty, adding unpredictability and challenge. This can take the form of dice rolls or shuffled cards, ensuring that no player has an unfair advantage.

We zoom in on games because they represent one of the most prevalent voluntary activities that engage our mental faculties.

According to a report by Newzoo,[3] a leading provider of market intelligence for the gaming industry, there were approximately 2.7 billion gamers worldwide in 2020, accounting for around one-third of the global population. The report defines a gamer as anyone who plays a video game on any device for any amount of time.

Furthermore, the global gaming market is projected to generate over $175 billion in revenue in 2021, with mobile gaming as the largest segment. Geographically, Asia-Pacific leads as the largest gaming market, followed by North America and Europe.

In a research study conducted by Entertainment Software Association (ESA),[4] 43% of adults aged 18–34 reported playing video games regularly, compared to 29% of those aged 35–44 and 22% of adults aged 45 and older.

Furthermore, ESA data revealed that 62% of all Americans play video games, with a slightly higher percentage of men (63%) than women (59%) engaging in gaming.

So, are games simply an escape from the harsh realities of the world, a form of relaxation, or something more profound?

For me, video games became a realm of profound fulfillment. Looking back, I realize the hard work and struggles I encountered while progressing in games, but it was all part of the exhilaration. It was an experience that brought me extreme joy.

But let's return to our topic of work. Is work the antithesis of games? Fortunately, it isn't. In her thought-provoking book, *Reality Is Broken: Why Games Make Us Better and How They Can Change the World*,[5] author and game design expert Jane McGonigal argues that the opposite of work is depression and that the game industry fulfills our need for better hard work. It's a fascinating concept.

McGonigal delves into the potential of games to enhance our lives and address real-world problems. She asserts that games are not just a form of entertainment but a powerful tool for boosting motivation, fostering creativity, and strengthening social connections. Moreover, she suggests that games can be harnessed to tackle significant social and environmental challenges, such as poverty, climate change, and public health.

To support her arguments, McGonigal draws upon a rich array of scientific research, historical examples, and her own experience in game design and play. She explores the psychological aspects of games and how they tap into our intrinsic desires for meaning, autonomy, and mastery. She also outlines practical strategies for incorporating game design principles into our daily lives and work, highlighting ways in which game designers can create more meaningful and impactful games.

And so, we find ourselves standing at the intersection of games and work, realizing that they are not mutually exclusive. In Chapter 8, we will delve beneath the surface to uncover the mechanisms through which games evoke emotions and explore how we can apply these insights to the realm of work. Games offer us hope and possibilities, and we are about to unlock their transformative potential.

Needs: the intersection of intrinsic motivations and the changing nature of work

Abraham Maslow's hierarchy of needs, a well-known theory in psychology, outlines the basic needs of human beings. Published in 1943 in a paper titled "A theory of human motivation,"[6] Maslow's hierarchy suggests that humans have physiological, safety, love/belonging, esteem, and self-actualization needs that must be fulfilled in a specific order.

Recent neurological research has shed light on how these needs are processed in the brain. For instance, the hypothalamus, often referred to as the "command center," regulates basic physiological needs like hunger and thirst. The amygdala and hippocampus are involved in processing safety and security needs, storing memories associated with danger and safety. Social and emotional needs, such as love and belonging, are processed in the limbic system, specifically in the cingulate cortex and insula, which regulate emotions and foster empathy and social awareness.

When it comes to esteem needs, the prefrontal cortex comes into play. This region of the brain handles executive functioning, including decision-making, goal-setting, and self-reflection. Self-actualization needs, on the other hand, are processed by the brain's default mode network, responsible for introspection, self-reflection, and creativity.

It's important to note that these functions involve intricate interactions and connections among various brain regions, and the relationship between the hierarchy of needs and the brain is still an active area of research with many unanswered questions.

Intrinsic motivations, rooted in our fundamental psychological needs, drive us to engage in specific activities. These motivations provide a sense of fulfillment and satisfaction independent of external rewards or incentives. Some of these intrinsic motivations include:

- **The desire for learning and intellectual challenge,** which compels us to seek out new experiences and engage in activities that foster personal growth and development.

- **The drive for achievement and success,** which motivates us to perform at a high level and strive for specific goals or standards. It encompasses the need for recognition, validation, and a sense of accomplishment.

- **The need for autonomy and control,** which fuels the desire to have agency over our lives and make our own decisions.

- **The longing for connection and a sense of belonging,** driving us to seek out activities that foster relationships and create a sense of community.

Mastery, the innate drive to master new skills and abilities, is believed to be related to the brain's reward system, which releases chemicals like dopamine, a neurotransmitter associated with feelings of pleasure and satisfaction, when we successfully learn and achieve. Desire for mastery, on the other hand, refers to the drive to improve one's skills and abilities, experience a sense of achievement, and master a particular domain. It is driven by a love of learning, personal growth, and a sense of purpose.

Research suggests that intrinsic motivation for achievement is associated with increased activity in the striatum, a region of the brain involved in reward processing and motivation. This motivation is believed to be linked to the release of dopamine.

Desire for mastery, on the other hand, is associated with increased activity in the hippocampus, a region involved in learning and memory. This motivation is thought to be related to the release of brain-derived neurotrophic factor (BDNF), a neurochemical crucial for neuron growth and survival, which is associated with long-term learning and memory.

Intrinsic motivations for achievement and desire for mastery can contribute to success and performance. However, the former often focuses on external outcomes and recognition, while the latter is more centered on internal processes and personal satisfaction.

Daniel Pink's book, *Drive: The Surprising Truth About What Motivates Us*,[7] explores the power of autonomy, mastery, and purpose. Pink presents an in-depth discussion of these concepts and their significance in motivating and fulfilling work and life. Drawing on extensive research and interviews with experts, he refers to this upgraded approach as "Motivation 3.0," surpassing primitive survival Motivation 1.0 and the reward-based Motivation 2.0 commonly found in many businesses.

Pink argues that traditional carrot-and-stick approaches to motivation are becoming outdated and fail to address the needs of modern, creative, and innovative workplaces. He emphasizes the growing importance of intrinsic motivation, where individuals are self-motivated by the freedom to pursue work they enjoy. In today's environments, where routine tasks are often outsourced, fostering innovation and creativity becomes essential. Allowing people to thrive by engaging in work they are passionate about is crucial.

Autonomy, mastery, and purpose are three core intrinsic needs. Autonomy pertains to being in control of our lives and decision-making. Mastery involves continuously improving our skills and becoming experts in our field. Purpose relates to a sense of belonging to something greater than ourselves, having a meaningful reason for being.

These intrinsic motivations can be traced back to the types of games we played as children. Autonomy is reflected in games that allow players to make choices and navigate through the game world. Mastery is observed in games that require learning new skills and strategies for progression. Purpose is found in games that inspire players to save the world or overcome challenges.

Understanding these intrinsic motivations enables us to create more engaging and motivating work experiences. By incorporating game-like elements into work, we can move beyond mere compliance and tap into the intrinsic motivations that stem from self-determination and personal growth.

Daniel Pink's motivational blueprint for modern work highlights the need to upgrade an outdated operating system. In the late 1990s, work primarily revolved around routine or algorithmic tasks, focusing on incremental improvements in speed, cost, and quality. However, with the rise of the internet economy, the nature of work underwent a significant shift.

The internet economy, estimated to be worth $15 trillion globally and contributing over 20% of global GDP, has been growing two and a half times faster than the physical world GDP. In Southeast Asia alone, a region with a population of 700 million, the internet economy is projected to reach $1 trillion within the next decade.[8]

Routine work is often outsourced in this new landscape, while problem-solving, collaboration, creativity, and service operational work require a physical presence. The demands of the modern workforce necessitate an upgrade to the old operating system that no longer meets the requirements of these new work types.

In Chapter 8, we will explore how the principles of games and intrinsic motivations can be applied to work, transforming it into a more engaging and fulfilling experience. The internet economy has provided us with new possibilities, and it is time to leverage these opportunities for the betterment of work and our overall well-being.

Summary

Chapter 7 explores the intersection of games and intrinsic motivations, offering a ray of hope in the changing landscape of work. Intrinsic motivations are identified as the core desires that drive us, including the need for learning, achievement, autonomy, connection, mastery, and purpose. Games are seen as a powerful tool to tap into these motivations, providing fulfillment and satisfaction independent of external rewards.

The chapter introduces Abraham Maslow's hierarchy of needs and the neurological processes associated with each need. It highlights Daniel Pink's book, *Drive*, which explores autonomy, mastery, and purpose as crucial elements for motivation and fulfillment in work and life. The concept of Motivation 3.0 is introduced as an upgrade to outdated motivational approaches.

The changing nature of work, influenced by the internet economy, is discussed, emphasizing the need to align work with intrinsic motivations. The chapter concludes by emphasizing the significance of intrinsic motivations in guiding individuals toward work that aligns with their innate drivers.

Overall, the chapter emphasizes the power of intrinsic motivations and games in shaping fulfilling work experiences. It highlights the importance of understanding and leveraging these motivations to create engaging and meaningful work environments.

Notes

1. Jesse Schell, *The Art of Game Design* (Boca Raton, FL: CRC Press, 2008).
2. Elliot Avedon and Brian Sutton-Smith, *The Study of Games* (Hoboken, NJ: Wiley, 1971).
3. Newzoo. (2020). Global games market report 2020. https://newzoo.com/resources/blog/newzoo-games-market-numbers-revenues-and-audience-2020-2023
4. Entertainment Software Association (ESA). (2021). Essential facts about the video game industry. https://www.theesa.com/resource/2021-essential-facts-about-the-video-game-industry/.
5. Jane McGonigal, *Reality Is Broken: Why Games Make Us Better and How They Can Change the World* (New York: Vintage, 2012).
6. Abraham Maslow, A theory of human motivation. *Psychological Review*, 50(1) (1943): 370–396.
7. Daniel Pink, *Drive: The Surprising Truth About What Motivates Us* (Edinburgh: Canongate Books, 2011).
8. Google, Temasek, and Bain & Company. E-Conomy SEA. (2021). Roaring 20's: The SEA digital decade. Google. https://www.bain.com/insights/e-conomy-sea-2021/

CHAPTER 8
GAME TIME, GAME TYPE

Discovering work suitability through games

What if games could serve as a guide to finding work that suits us best? This chapter aims to explore this question and uncover the underlying motivations that drive our game choices.

While we all have our individual reasons for playing games, whether it's to unwind after work or pass the time during the week, there is a deeper essence to why and how we play. By delving into the core motivations and values that drive us, we can identify patterns closely linked to our unique motivations, providing us with valuable insights.

Unlike work, games offer a multitude of choices that are much more fluid. Initially, we may be influenced by the games available to us, such as those owned by our older siblings, significant others, or our parents. However, over time, we naturally gravitate towards games that align with our personal preferences. The process of choosing specific games serves as a powerful compass for understanding what truly motivates us.

This aligns with the findings of the self-determination theory research we explored earlier, which revealed that, when given autonomy, we self-select choices that reflect our authentic selves. While short-term factors like circumstances, available options, and marketing messages may temporarily sway our decisions, in the long run, we naturally converge toward choices that define us.

Therefore, it is crucial to examine the longer-term patterns of our choices, with minimal constraints, in order to gain a clear glimpse into our default personality.

To start our exploration, let's consider if there are distinct types of players. Psychologists specializing in games have conducted remarkable research in this area and have developed a taxonomy that can guide us in answering our key questions.

One of the most frequently referenced works on player types is Bartle's taxonomy,[1] which describes four types of players in online Multi-user Dungeon games (the predecessors of today's massively multiplayer online role-playing games).

Now, let's examine the motivations that drive us to play specific games. Extensive research has explored the link between the games we choose to play and our intrinsic motivations. Self-determination theory (SDT) and related frameworks, such as Deci and Ryan's[2] intrinsic motivation theory, have been instrumental in this research.

SDT proposes that people's engagement in activities is driven by three fundamental psychological needs: autonomy, competence, and relatedness. Studies have found that people are more motivated to play games that align with these needs, and games that provide a sense of autonomy, competence, and relatedness tend to be more engaging and enjoyable.

Deci and Ryan's intrinsic motivation theory suggests that individuals are naturally motivated to engage in activities that are interesting, enjoyable, and fulfilling. When people participate in activities that align with their needs for autonomy, competence, and relatedness, they experience greater intrinsic motivation compared to activities that do not fulfill those needs.

Furthermore, research has indicated that games with strong narrative components tend to be more engaging for players who seek self-expression and creativity. On the other hand, games centered around skill-based mechanics tend to captivate players driven by the desire for challenge and achievement.

By understanding these connections between game preferences and intrinsic motivations, we can gain valuable insights into our own motivations and apply them to the realm of work. Games can serve as a guide, helping us uncover work that aligns with our authentic selves, providing us with a sense of fulfillment and motivation.

During my research, I had the opportunity to speak with a founder of a pre-IPO startup in Singapore. He shared an interesting insight from his interview process, where he asks candidates about the sports they play and why. By carefully listening to their responses and observing whether they emphasize individual aspects of the sports and their natural enjoyment, he gains valuable insights into their intrinsic motivations. While he admitted that it was more of a conversation starter and he had not tracked the longer-term correlation and success at work, it sparked an intriguing connection between game preferences and work suitability.

To further our understanding, let's explore the renowned Bartle's taxonomy of player types. Through extensive research of thousands of gamers, Bartle distilled distinct gamer personality clusters. The taxonomy includes four main types: Achiever, Explorer, Socializer, and Challenger. Each type possesses unique traits and intrinsic motivations that drive their gaming experiences:

- **The Achiever** gaming personality is motivated by the desire to demonstrate mastery and achieve success within the virtual world. They are driven by tangible rewards and recognition, and they are willing to invest significant time and effort to attain their goals.

- **Explorers,** on the other hand, are driven by the thirst for knowledge and the desire to uncover every facet of a game and its world, including its governing rules. Explorers prioritize the joy of discovery over tangible rewards and recognition. They immerse themselves fully in the game world, investing considerable time and effort in their exploratory endeavors.

- **Socializers** find their intrinsic motivation in socializing and connecting with others. They enjoy games that facilitate interaction, relationship-building, and community participation. For them, the social experience of playing the game takes precedence over winning or losing.

- **Challengers**, previously referred to as "killers," thrive on games that allow them to showcase their skills and compete against others. They are attracted to games with clear rules, objectives, and direct competition. PvP (player versus player) elements often captivate them, providing a platform to demonstrate their abilities and emerge victorious.

- **Hybrids** represent a unique blend of all the previous gamer types, seamlessly moving between different gaming motivations without a single dominant type.

Now that we have identified the gamer personality types, it is crucial to take a closer look at each dominant type to gain a deeper understanding of their natural motivations. To facilitate comprehension, we will explore popular games that align with each gamer personality, including both recent titles and timeless classics. We will also include non-video game references, recognizing that not all individuals engage in computer games.

Feel free to skim through the following pages to identify the gamer personality type that resonates most with you. You can return to this section later when seeking to assess someone's gamer personality and discover their underlying motivations.

Understanding these gamer personality types will prove fundamental in uncovering the intrinsic motivations of each subgroup, ultimately guiding us toward discovering work that aligns with our authentic selves.

The Achiever

John, a driven property agent known for his professionalism and dedication, possesses a hidden side that comes to life in the virtual realm. In his free time, John embarks on thrilling adventures in a virtual world, where he can escape the constraints of reality and truly shine. He spends hours playing his favorite game, Call of Duty, where he can engage in intense multiplayer battles and track his progress through various rankings and leaderboards.

Despite his composed demeanor, John possesses a fierce competitive streak and an unwavering drive to improve and succeed. When he's not assisting clients or scouting properties, John can often be found immersed in his game, pushing himself to new heights and testing his skills against others. To John, video games are not just a form of entertainment, but a way to challenge himself and experience the thrill of victory.

As an achiever, John sets clear goals within the game and relentlessly pursues them. He is highly motivated by tangible rewards and recognition, and he willingly invests time and effort to achieve his objectives. Whether it's solving a puzzle, acquiring items, or completing a level, John's intrinsic motivation drives him to attain high scores, complete tasks, and collect in-game achievements and awards.

John is meticulous and detail-oriented, carefully strategizing and perfecting his gameplay. He relishes the sense of accomplishment that comes from overcoming difficult challenges and tasks. His persistence is evident as he replays levels or missions multiple times, striving for perfection and achieving his desired results.

Achiever gamers like John are drawn to a variety of game types that align with their motivation for competition, mastery, and goal attainment.

The types of games that achievers gravitate toward include:

- **Sports games:** Basketball, football, or soccer simulators that offer clear goals and objectives, as well as opportunities for competition and mastery.

- **Puzzle games:** Engaging challenges like Tetris or Candy Crush that provide clear objectives and opportunities for competition and mastery.

- **Role-playing games (RPGs):** Games such as Final Fantasy or World of Warcraft that offer clear goals, character development, and opportunities for multiplayer competition.

- **Strategy games:** Titles like Civilization or Age of Empires that provide clear goals, empire-building challenges, and multiplayer competition.

- **First-person shooters (FPS):** Immersive games like Call of Duty or Halo that offer clear objectives, opportunities for competition, and different game modes to achieve victory.

In the 1990s, some of the most popular achiever games included:

- **Super Mario Bros.:** A classic platformer game with challenging levels and hidden secrets to uncover.

- **Doom:** A fast-paced first-person shooter known for its adrenaline-fueled gameplay and a wide range of achievements and challenges.

- **Tetris:** A simple yet addictive puzzle game focused on achieving high scores and mastering the gameplay.

- **The Legend of Zelda: A Link to the Past:** An action-adventure game with challenging dungeons, secrets, and collectible items.

- **Street Fighter II:** A competitive fighting game with a diverse cast of characters, each with unique abilities and moves.

In the 2000s, notable achiever games include:

- **Fortnite:** A popular battle royale game offering fast-paced survival gameplay, challenges, and achievements.

- **Apex Legends:** A battle royale game emphasizing skill demonstration, mastery, and cosmetic rewards.

- **Player Unknown's Battlegrounds (PUBG):** A tactical battle royale game with intense matches, achievements, and cosmetic items.

- **Grand Theft Auto V:** An open-world action game featuring a range of activities, missions, races, and rewards.

- **The Witcher 3: Wild Hunt:** An immersive action RPG with challenging gameplay and opportunities for mastery.

Achievers aren't limited to video games alone. Even non-video games can provide a platform for their competitive nature, such as:

- **Monopoly:** A classic board game known for its competitive gameplay, property management, and wealth accumulation.

- **Settlers of Catan:** A strategy game where players build settlements, trade resources, and compete for control.

By understanding the preferences and motivations of achievers like John, we can gain insights into their natural inclinations and discover how to align their intrinsic motivations with suitable work environments.

The Explorer

Introducing Jessy, an accountant by day and an intrepid explorer in the virtual world of The Elder Scrolls. She craves the excitement and freedom that come with venturing into uncharted territories, battling mythical creatures, and uncovering hidden treasures. With each new journey, Jessy feels a rush of anticipation, always eager to discover what wonders await her.

Let's go deeper into the world of Explorer gamers and the types of games that captivate their adventurous spirits:

Sandbox games:

- **Minecraft:** An open-ended game that allows players to unleash their creativity and build anything they can imagine.

- **Grand Theft Auto:** Provides a sprawling cityscape for players to freely explore and engage in various activities.

Open-World games:

- **The Elder Scrolls:** Immersive fantasy worlds like Skyrim or Morrowind offer vast landscapes, intriguing quests, and countless secrets to uncover.

- **Assassin's Creed:** Historical settings like Ancient Egypt or Renaissance Italy provide immersive environments for exploration, parkour, and stealthy adventures.

Adventure games:

- **The Legend of Zelda:** A beloved franchise known for its captivating storylines, challenging puzzles, and expansive worlds waiting to be discovered.
- **Monkey Island:** A classic point-and-click adventure series filled with humor, intriguing characters, and captivating quests.

Simulation games:

- **The Sims:** Allows players to create and manage virtual lives, experimenting with various scenarios and uncovering the consequences of their choices.
- **Kerbal Space Program:** Offers a realistic space simulation experience, allowing players to build and launch their own rockets, explore celestial bodies, and embark on interplanetary missions.

Exploration games:

- **Abzû:** Immerses players in a visually stunning underwater world, inviting them to uncover its mysteries and encounter diverse marine life.
- **Journey:** A mesmerizing adventure where players traverse vast deserts, encountering other travelers and unraveling the secrets of a mysterious world.

Open-World board games:

- **Risk:** A classic strategy game that lets players conquer territories and engage in global conflicts on a world map.

- **Betrayal at Baldur's Gate:** A cooperative board game where players explore a haunted city, encountering monsters and solving mysteries.

Adventure board games:

- **Clue or Cluedo:** Players become detectives, solving a murder mystery by exploring rooms, gathering clues, and identifying the culprit.
- **Mystery of the Abbey:** Set in a medieval abbey, players investigate a series of mysterious events and work together to uncover the truth.

Simulation board games:

- **Agricola:** Players take on the role of farmers, managing their resources, expanding their farms, and striving for prosperity.
- **Charterstone:** A legacy-style board game that allows players to build and develop a unique village over multiple play sessions.

Exploration board games:

- **Pandemic:** Players work together to combat a global pandemic, strategizing and traveling the world to prevent the spread of diseases.
- **Spirit Island:** A cooperative game where players embody powerful spirits, defending an island from colonizers and exploring its mystical powers.

By understanding the motivations and preferences of Explorer gamers like Jessy, we can tap into their innate sense of curiosity and love for discovery. Incorporating elements of exploration, creativity, and immersive storytelling in work or other experiences can engage and inspire these individuals, allowing them to thrive in their natural element.

The Socializer

Introducing Alex, an enthusiastic and outgoing entrepreneur who thrives on forging connections and building communities. In addition to his business ventures, Alex finds solace and excitement in the world of multiplayer games, where he can engage in lively conversations, form alliances, and share laughter with friends and strangers alike. For Alex, gaming is not just a form of entertainment, it's a medium that allows him to nurture relationships and foster a vibrant sense of community.

Socializers like Alex view games as an avenue for social interaction and meaningful connections. They seek out experiences that enable them to engage with other players, share stories, and create lasting bonds. While they may not be driven by intense competition, socializers value cooperative and collaborative gameplay that encourages teamwork and shared experiences.

Now, let's explore the game types that socializers like Alex gravitate toward, where they can truly flourish and indulge in their social nature:

Multiplayer games: Fast-paced first-person shooters, exhilarating racing games, or exciting fighting games that offer real-time competition or cooperation with other players. These games provide socializers with the opportunity to connect with friends, form communities, and experience the joy of shared victories.

Party games: Titles like Mario Party or Rayman Raving Rabbids, specifically designed for group play and featuring a delightful collection of mini-games that can be enjoyed together. These games are perfect for social gatherings, igniting laughter, and fostering memorable experiences.

Online Role-Playing Games (RPGs): Immersive virtual worlds such as World of Warcraft and Final Fantasy XIV, where players can interact with each other, embark on epic quests, and collaborate in overcoming challenges. Socializers relish the camaraderie, shared adventures, and the opportunity to build meaningful relationships within the game.

Simulation games: Examples include The Sims or Animal Crossing, where players can create and manage their own virtual worlds, interact with other players, and cultivate a sense of community. Socializers appreciate the freedom to express their creativity, connect with others, and build relationships within the simulated environment.

Mobile games: Socializers find joy in games like Words with Friends or Draw Something, which provide opportunities to connect and play with people from anywhere, even asynchronously. These games offer convenient avenues for socialization and enjoyable interactions, catering to the busy lives of entrepreneurs like Alex.

During the 1990s and 2000s, socializers likely found pleasure in games such as:

- **The Sims:** A beloved life simulation game series that allows players to express their creativity, interact with virtual characters, and foster social connections.

- **Mario Party:** A lively party game featuring a collection of mini-games designed for group play. It promises laughter, friendly competition, and enjoyable experiences for socializers.

- **Super Mario Kart:** An exciting racing game that can be played with friends, combining both competition and cooperation. Socializers relished the exhilarating races and shared moments of triumph.

In recent years, popular games among socializers include:

- **Fortnite:** A globally popular battle royale game known for its fast-paced gameplay, humor, and robust social features that foster connections and create shared experiences among players.

- **Among Us:** A multiplayer party game that challenges players to socialize, interact, and engage in deduction, resulting in thrilling and entertaining gameplay that brings socializers together.

- **Roblox:** An expansive online game platform and creation system that offers a wide range of games and opportunities for social interaction. It caters to players of all ages, allowing socializers to connect, collaborate, and unleash their creativity.

- **Call of Duty: Modern Warfare:** A gripping first-person shooter that provides socializers with the thrill of competition and the chance to forge alliances with other players.

As an entrepreneur, Alex finds that gaming not only offers an escape but also serves as a catalyst for networking and building relationships that extend beyond the virtual realm. Gaming allows him to nurture connections, share experiences, and tap into the power of community, enhancing his entrepreneurial spirit.

The Challenger

Meet Ana, an events manager who thrives on pushing herself to new limits. When she's not organizing and coordinating events, Ana immerses herself in her favorite strategy game, constantly seeking out challenges and refining her tactics. Her unwavering determination is not only evident in the virtual world but also in her approach to planning and executing successful events, where she conquers unexpected obstacles with gusto.

Challengers are drawn to games that offer a high level of difficulty, requiring intense focus and quick reflexes. They are motivated by the thrill of competition and the satisfaction of overcoming obstacles and defeating opponents. Ana embodies these characteristics as she embraces challenges both in her virtual gaming adventures and in her real-life endeavors as an events manager.

While achievers and challengers share a drive for competition and winning, there are notable differences between these personality types. Challengers seek the adrenaline rush that comes from facing daunting challenges and engaging in intense competition. They relish the opportunity to demonstrate their skills and defeat opponents, driven by the desire for recognition, prestige, and the thrill of victory.

During the 1990s and 2000s, challengers found themselves drawn to games such as:

- **Street Fighter II:** This influential fighting game allowed players to engage in one-on-one combat, testing their mastery of various moves and strategies. The competitive nature of the game appealed to challengers who sought direct competition and the chance to showcase their gaming skills.

- **StarCraft:** A real-time strategy game that required players to manage resources while outmaneuvering opponents. With its deep strategic elements and competitive multiplayer mode, StarCraft provided challengers with a platform to demonstrate their competitive spirit and mastery of the game.

- **Counter-Strike:** A first-person shooter game that demanded strategy, teamwork, and quick reflexes. Counter-Strike's objective-based gameplay, where teams competed in defusing bombs or rescuing hostages, catered to the challenger's love for competition and skill-based challenges.

More recently, challengers have found themselves drawn to games such as:

- **Overwatch:** A team-based first-person shooter game emphasizing coordination and strategy. Players select unique heroes with distinct abilities, working together to secure objectives. The competitive mode, featuring ranked performance, provides a fitting challenge for Ana's competitive nature.

- **Player Unknown's Battlegrounds (PUBG):** A battle royale game where up to 100 players fight in a last-man-standing deathmatch. Players scavenge for weapons and supplies, strategizing to outlast and outsmart opponents. The intense competition and opportunity for mastery align well with Ana's challenger archetype.

- **Valorant:** A tactical first-person shooter game featuring unique agents with abilities. Teams compete to plant or defuse a bomb, requiring strategic thinking, quick reflexes, and precise aim. The high level of competition and opportunity for mastery appeal to Ana's intrinsic motivation as a challenger.

These games are characterized by fast-paced action, real-time competition, and the need for quick reflexes and strategic thinking. They offer challengers the chance to test their skills, achieve recognition, and experience the exhilaration of victory. Additionally, the battle royale genre has gained popularity among challengers for its intense multiplayer battles and the thrill of survival.

In the realm of board games, chess stands as the absolute favorite for challengers. This classic game of strategy and tactics pits players against each other in a head-to-head battle of wits, with the ultimate goal of checkmating the opponent's king. The intricate strategies and endless possibilities for outmaneuvering opponents perfectly align with the challenger personality, making chess a natural choice for those seeking mental challenges and intense competition.

The Hybrid

Prepare to meet Andrew, a computer engineer with a boundless range of interests and skills. His love for video games perfectly reflects his versatile nature. Andrew is a true jack-of-all-trades, always up for a challenge and eager to dive into something new. Whether it's a heart-pounding first-person shooter or a complex strategy game, he embraces the opportunity to explore and experiment.

Andrew possesses a deep appreciation for games that offer him the chance to delve into different genres and experiences. He finds just as much satisfaction spending hours immersed in a captivating role-playing game as he does honing his skills in a competitive shooter. His curiosity and thirst for knowledge drive him to embrace the diversity that gaming has to offer.

But what truly sets Andrew apart is his unwavering belief in the power of games to bring people together. He cherishes opportunities to play with friends and strangers alike, finding immense joy in the social connections that gaming provides. Whether he's competing against others or cooperating with them, Andrew thrives on the sense of community and camaraderie that gaming fosters. For him, video games transcend mere entertainment—they are a gateway to exploration, personal growth, and meaningful connections.

Andrew embodies the essence of a hybrid gamer, with a balanced intrinsic motivational profile that makes it difficult to pinpoint a dominant motivation. His engagement with games reflects his unique personality, showcasing a diverse range of interests and an open-mindedness to explore various gaming experiences. While some may perceive this as indecisiveness, Andrew's deep immersion and genuine passion in each game he plays demonstrate the depth of his engagement and his ability to embrace the multifaceted nature of gaming.

So, next time you encounter a hybrid gamer like Andrew, appreciate their ability to traverse different gaming worlds with enthusiasm and an eagerness to explore the unknown. They are the true adventurers of the gaming realm, seeking challenges, connecting with others, and finding their own extraordinary path within the vast landscape of gaming possibilities.

Motivation profiles of gamers

As we delve deeper into understanding intrinsic motivation, it becomes evident that the games we play offer valuable insights into our intrinsic motivational profiles. To truly comprehend these motivations, we need to go one level deeper and ask ourselves the following questions:

What do you enjoy the most about the game? By identifying the specific aspects of a game that bring us joy and fulfillment, we can uncover the underlying intrinsic motivations that drive our engagement. Is it the sense of accomplishment when completing challenging tasks? The thrill of competition and victory? The opportunity to connect and collaborate with others? Understanding what we enjoy the most provides valuable clues about our intrinsic motivations.

Do the games we play change with age? It is intriguing to observe that the games we play indeed evolve as we grow older. Different age groups exhibit distinct preferences and interests when it comes to gaming. Let's explore some examples:

- **Kids aged 7–9:** This is the age of reason, where children develop their cognitive abilities and independence. They become more discerning in their choices of toys and games, actively selecting those that align with their interests and preferences.

- **Tweens aged 10–13:** This period marks significant neurological growth, allowing children to think more deeply and passionately about their interests. They may develop obsessions and exhibit heightened enthusiasm for specific types of games.

- **Teens aged 13–18:** Adolescence is a time of preparation for adulthood. While there may be gender differences in interests, all teens are eager to experiment with new experiences, some of which are fulfilled through gameplay.

- **Young adults aged 18–24:** As young adults, individuals have established their preferences and tastes in games and entertainment. With more time and disposable income, they become avid consumers of games.

Throughout our teenage years, our gaming preferences tend to solidify, aligning with the formation of our personalities. By our early twenties, our game profile typically stabilizes.

Coincidentally, this period corresponds to the peak influence of the self-determination theory, allowing us to gain a comprehensive understanding of our intrinsic motivations.

By recognizing the correlation between age and gaming preferences, we can gain valuable insights into the intrinsic motivations that drive our engagement with games. Understanding these motivations is key to unlocking our true potential and aligning our pursuits with our core desires.

Behind our choices of games

Choosing which games to play is like embarking on a journey through the labyrinth of our intrinsic motivations. It's a complex dance between our desires, external influences, and the mysterious workings of our own minds. While we may think we have full control over our choices, there's a hidden symphony of thoughts and emotions guiding us.

In this grand game of game selection, marketers wield their power, weaving intricate spells with their catchy ads and persuasive promises. They tap into our deepest desires, using behavioral psychology to entice us to part with our hard-earned money. But are we truly the masters of our decisions, or merely pawns in their grand design?

Recommendations from family and friends whisper in our ears, planting seeds of curiosity and intrigue. Online reviews beckon us, promising tales of epic adventures and immersive worlds. Yet, even as we rely on external guidance, there's an internal compass guiding us toward games that resonate with our intrinsic motivations.

Uncovering these motivations is like unraveling the secrets of a treasure map. One approach is to directly ask individuals about their passions, interests, and dreams. But beware! This path is fraught with challenges, as social expectations and the desire to fit a certain work profile can cloud our true desires. We may find ourselves crafting responses that please others rather than revealing our authentic selves.

Observation becomes our ally, allowing us to witness the sparks of genuine enthusiasm and sustained interest. By observing individuals in different settings, we catch glimpses of their inner fire, their true motivations shining through. Yet, even this path has its limitations. How can we truly understand someone's intrinsic motivations without diving deep into the rich tapestry of their past experiences and behaviors?

We yearn for a scalable solution, a way to unlock the mysteries of intrinsic motivation in the context of work. But can we truly gage someone's self-driven passions by simply surveying their sense of autonomy? The answers we receive may be skewed, influenced by the desire to please or conform, obscuring the raw truth beneath a veil of social expectations.

So, as we navigate the labyrinth of game selection and uncover the enigma of intrinsic motivations, let us tread with caution. Let us seek genuine self-expression, allowing individuals to reveal their true desires without fear of judgment. Only then can we glimpse the shimmering core of their motivations and forge a path toward meaningful engagement and fulfillment.

In this game of understanding, the rules are still being written, and the playing field is ever-evolving. But the quest to uncover intrinsic motivations continues, a thrilling adventure that challenges our assumptions and inspires new possibilities.

Unveiling the mystery of team games and teamwork

In the quest for effective teamwork, a captivating question arises: *Can playing team-based games transform us into stellar team players in the workplace?* This intriguing inquiry prompted a startup founder to delve deeper into the matter, incorporating it into his job interviews. Curiosity sparked, he sought to uncover the link between gaming and teamwork prowess.

Assembling a high-performing team is an art form, and experts in the fields of teamwork and organizational behavior have identified communication, responsiveness, and adaptability as key attributes for success. Extensive research studies, such as McChrystal et al., *Team of Teams*, and Lencioni, *The Five Dysfunctions of a* Team,[3] have shed light on these critical factors.

The startup founder's unique approach involved exploring candidates' involvement in team sports and delving into their motivations behind such activities. His hypothesis was that playing team games could potentially cultivate the necessary skills for effective teamwork in a professional setting.

However, the quest for answers led to intriguing findings. While team-based games provide an opportunity to practice and develop certain teamwork skills, such as communication, collaboration, and problem-solving, they do not necessarily translate into enhanced team member effectiveness in the workplace. The connection between gaming as a team and excelling in a team setting at work proved to be elusive.

The realm of gaming, although offering a platform for honing certain teamwork skills, encompasses a unique context that may differ significantly from the complexities and dynamics of real-world team collaborations. While games may foster elements of communication and cooperation, the intricate interplay of personalities, diverse perspectives, and organizational structures in the workplace add an additional layer of complexity that cannot be fully replicated within the confines of a game.

Thus, it becomes apparent that playing team games alone is not a definitive predictor of an individual's performance within a team at work. The journey toward effective teamwork calls for a holistic approach, considering various factors, such as individual traits, experiences, and adaptability to the specific work environment.

In the ever-evolving landscape of team dynamics, the quest for optimal collaboration continues. The exploration of the relationship between team games and workplace teamwork uncovers valuable insights and challenges conventional assumptions. As we navigate this uncharted territory, let us remain open to the possibilities, drawing inspiration from both the virtual realm of gaming and the real-world complexities of team interactions.

Unveiling the intricacies of gambling and its motivational aspects

The world of gambling has always fascinated me, particularly the allure of games of pure luck. After a few visits to Las Vegas, I found myself captivated not only by the abundance of slot machines and bustling casinos, but also by the countless individuals who were seemingly entranced by these games, playing fervently around the clock. Eager to unravel this mystery, I ventured into conversations with industry professionals—the masterminds behind the design of these captivating machines and games. To my surprise, I discovered that the real gambling empire had expanded from physical casinos to the vast realm of online gambling, offering unparalleled convenience to customers and multiplying profits.

Motivations for gambling vary among individuals, encompassing a range of factors, such as the thrill of taking risks, the allure of potential financial gain, the excitement derived from the games themselves, or the social aspect of gambling alongside others. For some, gambling serves as an escape from stress or negative emotions, while others turn to it as a means of coping with boredom or life's challenges. At its core, gambling entices our brains by presenting a tantalizing problem: how to navigate the realm of calculated risk and maximize financial gains.

Interestingly, concepts derived from the world of gambling can be applied to make operations work more enjoyable in a multitude of ways. One approach involves introducing elements of chance and uncertainty into operational tasks, injecting a sense of excitement and engagement. For instance, operations workers could be granted a set number of "points" to use when making strategic decisions or taking calculated risks, with the outcomes determined randomly and unpredictably. This approach offers a heightened sense of challenge, infusing operations work with enjoyment. Furthermore, workers could be rewarded with tangible or intangible prizes upon achieving specific goals or milestones, fostering a profound sense of accomplishment and satisfaction. By integrating elements reminiscent of gambling into operations work, we unlock the potential to make it a more rewarding and captivating experience for those involved.

The realm of online betting is an entity on its own. Throughout my research for this book, I engaged in conversations with numerous industry experts and delved into the inner workings of these games. I aimed to understand what entices individuals to continuously return, dedicating months to a seemingly simple, repetitive activity such as playing slot machines. My initial suspicion was not rooted in a sinister desire to create addiction in the workplace, but rather a genuine curiosity: *Could we gain insight into identifying individuals with a natural inclination toward operational work?*

Slot gaming constitutes a substantial subsegment within the gaming industry, and the statistics astounded me. Online gaming alone boasts 3,500 operator sites, 41,000 games, and 650 game studios.[4] Approximately 500 new games are launched each month, with numerous experiments conducted to create captivating games that retain users for extended periods.

Determining what makes a game exceptional boils down to the mechanics of reward. Does it offer frequent small rewards or less frequent, substantial rewards? Additionally, factors such as layout, colors, and themes (such as Aztec, animal, or Irish motifs, for inexplicable reasons) influence players' preferences and engagement.

In the book, *Addiction by Design: Machine Gambling in Las Vegas*,[5] anthropologist Natasha Dow Schüll delves into the rise of machine gambling and its impact on people's lives. She uncovers how modern slot machines and electronic gambling machines are meticulously designed to engross players and maintain a state of continuous play. These machines are programmed to provide variable rewards and create an illusion of control, despite the casino always holding the odds in its favor. Consequently, players may become immersed in the machines, persistently playing even when faced with losses or negative consequences.

Schüll highlights the addictive nature of machine gambling, with some players spending hours or even days consecutively engrossed in the games. She notes that these machines are often situated in highly stimulating environments, complete with bright lights, captivating sounds, and other sensory cues meticulously crafted to keep players engaged. Moreover, she suggests that machine gambling appeals to individuals seeking an escape from their problems, as it offers a sense of excitement and control that may be absent from their daily lives.

While gaming executives have repeatedly emphasized that addiction is detrimental to their business, as it depletes customers' savings and discourages their return, the practical implementation of measures to prevent addiction remains somewhat elusive.

Online gaming, although a potential proxy for operational work, presents challenges in building long-term sustainable engagement and avoiding the creation of workaholism.

As we navigate the intricate realm of gambling and its motivational aspects, it is crucial to weigh up the opportunities and potential pitfalls associated with applying these principles to various domains of life. Striking a delicate balance between captivation and addiction, we can harness the allure of games of chance to enhance our understanding of human motivation and strive for more fulfilling experiences in both work and play.

Notes

1. R. A. Bartle, Hearts, clubs, diamonds, spades: Players who suit MUDs. *Journal of MUD Research*, 1(1) (1996): 19. https://mud.co.uk/richard/hcds.htm
2. E. L. Deci, and R. M. Ryan, *Intrinsic Motivation and Self-Determination in Human Behavior* (New York: Plenum Press. 1985).
3. S. McChrystal, T. Collins, D. Silverman, and C. Fussell, *Team of Teams: New Rules of Engagement for a Complex World* (New York: Portfolio/Penguin, 2015); P. Lencioni, *The Five Dysfunctions of a Team: A Leadership Fable* (San Francisco: Jossey-Bass. 2002).
4. Grand View Research. (2023). Global online gambling market. https://www.grandviewresearch.com/industry-analysis/online-gambling-market
5. Natasha Dow Schüll, *Addiction by Design: Machine Gambling in Las Vegas* (Princeton, NJ: Princeton University Press, 2012).

PART III
THE SCIENCE OF MOTIVATION

CHAPTER 9
MOTIVATIONS

Why did we choose money as the primary motivator for work?

This question takes us on a journey through time, exploring the origins of monetary compensation and its impact on motivation. From ancient civilizations to modern societies, the allure of money has shaped our perception of work and its rewards.

In ancient Mesopotamia and Egypt, dating back to around 3000 BC, we find early indications of money being used as payment for labor. The Sumerians employed the "barley standard," paying workers in standardized amounts of barley that could be exchanged for other goods and services. Similarly, the Egyptians used a currency called "shat," which held value in grains and provided workers with the means to acquire essentials like food, clothing, and housing.

Money's role as a motivator for work operates at both the neurological and behavioral levels, requiring an exploration of the biological foundations of reward systems and the societal constructs that shape our behavior.

At the neurological level, we uncover the influence of dopamine, a neurotransmitter central to the brain's reward system. When we anticipate or receive a reward, such as money, dopamine is released in key brain regions, creating a pleasurable sensation and reinforcing the behaviors that led to the reward. Moreover, the prefrontal cortex, responsible for higher-order cognitive functions, plays a vital role in motivation. It becomes activated when we perceive money as a means to achieve desired outcomes, driving us to engage in goal-directed behavior.

On the behavioral level, money serves as a powerful positive reinforcer within the framework of operant conditioning. When individuals receive money for their work, they are more likely to repeat those actions in the future, having learned that they lead to positive outcomes. Expectancy theory further emphasizes the motivation that arises from the belief that effort, performance, and reward are strongly linked.

Money's impact extends beyond individual psychology and intertwines with social factors. It holds symbolic value in society, often associated with social status and success. The desire to maintain or improve one's standing within a social hierarchy can act as a potent motivator, as individuals compare their income and material possessions with those of their peers. Additionally, money plays a crucial role in meeting basic physiological needs, as outlined by Maslow's Hierarchy of Needs (see Chapter 7). By providing the means to satisfy these fundamental requirements, money becomes a critical motivator for work.

While money has historically been the primary motivator for work, it is essential to recognize its limitations. As the complexity and demand for skills increase, monetary compensation tends to rise. However, the intrinsic motivations that fuel creativity, innovation, and long-term satisfaction cannot be solely driven by financial rewards. Exploring alternative sources of motivation and understanding the multifaceted nature of human desires can lead to a more comprehensive understanding of what truly motivates individuals in their work.

Getting in the zone: exploring the power of flow in work and games

Have you ever been so engrossed in an activity that hours flew by in what felt like minutes? That state of complete absorption and focused engagement is what psychologists call "flow." It's that magical zone where we are fully immersed in a task that is both challenging and within our capabilities.

In Mihaly Csikszentmihalyi's groundbreaking book, *Flow: The Psychology of Optimal Experience*,[1] he delves into this concept that captivates our attention and brings immense satisfaction. Flow is characterized by deep enjoyment and an intense focus on the present moment. When we're in a state of flow, we become so absorbed in the activity that distractions fade away.

Achieving flow is not a matter of luck but rather a skill we can cultivate. It involves understanding and controlling the cognitive and emotional processes that govern our moments of happiness and unhappiness. The state of flow is often associated with work, where we can find ourselves fully absorbed and lose track of time. It's that feeling of being "in the zone" when we are completely focused on the task at hand.

The state of flow is not only desirable but also has practical implications for our work life. When we enter the flow state, we become highly productive and efficient. It's a state where creativity flourishes, and we can perform at our best. However, reaching and maintaining flow can be a challenge.

Interestingly, video game designers have long recognized the importance of flow in creating engaging experiences. They aim to design games that are "easy to learn and hard to master," drawing players in and keeping them engaged for longer periods. Our brains are wired for problem-solving, but they also have a finely-tuned mechanism to assess whether a problem is solvable or is too simple. Games that strike the right balance of challenge and skill captivate our attention, activating our reward centers and keeping us in the flow.

To help players achieve flow, game designers employ various techniques. They carefully balance the difficulty level of the game with the player's skill, ensuring that it remains engaging without becoming frustrating. Visual and audio cues provide feedback, helping players gage their progress and performance. Pacing, difficulty scaling, and player choice further enhance the immersive experience.

Research has shown that activities that are easy to learn but hard to master are the most engaging and enjoyable. These flow activities provide a sense of challenge and accomplishment that keeps us motivated and fulfilled. Whether it's sports, games, artistic pursuits, or intellectual challenges, these activities offer clear goals, immediate feedback, and a perfect balance of challenge and skill.

By harnessing the principles of flow, we can unlock our full potential, find joy in our tasks, and experience a profound sense of fulfillment.

Riding the waves of accomplishment: the science behind satisfaction and achievement

In the world of games, the concept of "easy to learn and hard to master" is a hallmark of successful designs. These games are intuitive and require minimal instructions, allowing players to dive right in and start enjoying the experience. Like an on-ramp to an exciting journey, they guide players through the learning process, equipping them with the necessary understanding and providing practice opportunities to hit the ground running.

But what makes these games truly captivating is their depth and complexity, which reveal themselves gradually over time. As players delve deeper into the game, they encounter challenges that test their skills and push them to improve. The journey toward mastery becomes an exhilarating pursuit, fueling a sense of accomplishment and satisfaction when players finally conquer the game's complexities.

Similarly, work can be designed to follow this concept, offering employees tasks and skills that are easy to grasp initially but challenging to master. By carefully considering the balance between task difficulty and skill level, work can be structured to provide a gradual learning curve, allowing employees to develop their expertise over time. Clear goals and immediate feedback play vital roles in maintaining motivation and focus, offering a sense of achievement as individuals progress in their work.

So, what makes the pursuit of challenging problems more appealing than solving simple ones? One reason may be the level of mental effort required. Simple problems often do not engage our minds as intensely as complex ones, leaving us with a sense of boredom and lack of interest. The sense of accomplishment and reward that comes with overcoming difficult challenges may also be lacking in simpler tasks, diminishing their appeal. Moreover, some individuals are naturally drawn to the thrill of tackling complex problems, finding simple tasks too easy to fully engage their minds.

The experience of accomplishment and satisfaction is not solely psychological; it is rooted in the intricate workings of our brains. When we successfully complete a task or achieve a goal, our brains release dopamine, a neurotransmitter associated with pleasure and reward. This release triggers a sense of satisfaction and accomplishment, fueling our motivation to pursue further goals. Additional neurotransmitters like serotonin and endorphins contribute to our overall sense of well-being and happiness. These chemical reactions in the brain provide the biological foundation for the psychological experience of accomplishment and satisfaction.

Imagine being completely engrossed in a game, where every obstacle is effortlessly overcome and every victory brings an indescribable joy. Hours fly by, and time seems to lose all meaning as you become one with the game. The feeling of being in the flow, completely focused and absorbed in the task at hand, becomes a profound and immersive experience. It's a state where the virtual world merges seamlessly with reality, and nothing else matters.

As you emerge from this state of flow, a sense of accomplishment and longing washes over you. You've achieved something significant, and a part of you yearns to return to that captivating realm. The connection between accomplishment, satisfaction, and the release of chemicals in the brain becomes evident, shaping our experiences in both games and work.

Understanding the science behind satisfaction and achievement opens doors to designing engaging experiences, both in games and in our professional lives. By embracing the principle of "easy to learn and hard to master," we can cultivate a sense of fulfillment, motivate ourselves to overcome challenges, and embark on journeys of continuous growth and accomplishment. So, let's dive into the exhilarating world of accomplishment and satisfaction, where the waves of success carry us to new heights.

Unveiling the brain's motivational machinery

Now, we take a closer look inside our brains to discover the intricate workings that drive our motivations. It all starts with the limbic system, often referred to as the "emotional brain." This group of brain structures plays a central role in regulating emotions, memories, and motivation. Two key players in the limbic system are the hippocampus and the amygdala.

The hippocampus, located in the temporal lobe, serves multiple important functions. It is responsible for memory formation and consolidation, helping us convert short-term memories into long-term ones. It also plays a role in spatial navigation, allowing us to remember and navigate through our surroundings. Furthermore, the hippocampus contributes to emotional regulation by processing emotional responses and memories. However, chronic stress and depression can negatively impact the hippocampus, leading to impaired memory and reduced cognitive function.

On the other hand, the amygdala, resembling an almond shape, influences the experiencing of emotions, especially fear and aggression. This powerhouse triggers the body's instinctive "fight or flight" response in the face of perceived threats, releasing hormones like adrenaline and cortisol to prepare us for action. Additionally, the amygdala plays a part in the formation and recall of emotional memories. Moreover, it is involved in regulating social behavior, including the processing of facial expressions and the modulation of social and emotional responses.

While the limbic system governs emotions and memories, the reward system takes charge of our motivation and decision-making processes. Composed of structures like the nucleus accumbens, the ventral tegmental area, and the prefrontal cortex, the reward system forms a network responsible for processing pleasurable experiences. When activated, it releases neurotransmitters like dopamine, which elicit feelings of pleasure and satisfaction. This process reinforces behaviors that are beneficial to our survival and overall well-being.

The reward system is an essential component of the brain's motivational machinery. It fuels our desires and drives us to engage in activities that bring us pleasure and reward. Dopamine is released in response to various experiences, such as enjoying a delicious meal or engaging in physical exercise. Additionally, dopamine is released when we achieve our goals or successfully complete tasks, fostering a sense of accomplishment and motivating us to pursue further objectives.

The brain's reward system operates on the principles of classical conditioning. Through repeated pairings of neutral stimuli with pleasurable experiences, the brain learns to associate the neutral stimuli with the release of dopamine. For example, if we consistently listen to a particular song while enjoying a certain food, the brain begins to link the song with the pleasure of eating, triggering the release of dopamine even when we only hear the song. This conditioned response demonstrates how our brain can be trained to release dopamine in anticipation of pleasurable stimuli.

By understanding the interplay between the limbic system and the reward system, we gain insights into the mechanisms that drive our motivations. These neurobiological processes shape our emotional experiences, memories, and the pursuit of pleasurable activities. As we unravel the secrets of our brain's motivational machinery, we can harness this knowledge to cultivate a deeper understanding of human motivation and enhance our own drive and fulfillment in both games and work.

Unleashing the power of intrinsic motivation

Let's delve into the fascinating world of classical conditioning and its relationship to intrinsic rewards. As discussed above, Russian psychologist Ivan Pavlov conducted a groundbreaking experiment with dogs, demonstrating the power of classical conditioning. This experiment revealed how neutral stimuli can become associated with pleasurable experiences, shaping our motivations and desires.

Classical conditioning plays a role in cultivating intrinsic rewards, which are the pleasurable feelings we experience when engaged in activities that are inherently enjoyable and interesting. These rewards are often associated with challenging tasks that require skill and mastery, such as playing a musical instrument or solving complex puzzles. Classical conditioning strengthens these intrinsic rewards by linking them with external stimuli. For example, if we consistently feel a sense of accomplishment and enjoyment when solving difficult puzzles while listening to a specific song, we may eventually associate the song itself with the intrinsic reward of solving puzzles. Our brain learns to release dopamine, in response to the song, even without the puzzle-solving context.

When it comes to games, they offer a window into our intrinsic motivations. The games we enjoy playing can reveal our psychological drives and interests. If we are drawn to games involving problem-solving or challenges, it may indicate a motivation to learn and grow. On the other hand, if we gravitate toward competitive games, it could signal a desire to achieve victory or excel.

Daniel Pink, in his book, *Drive: The Surprising Truth About What Motivates Us,*[2] introduces the concept of Motivation 2.0, which characterizes the traditional approach to work. Motivation 2.0 emphasizes extrinsic rewards like pay and employs a system of contingent rewards and punishments. It also grants a high degree of control over work tasks. However, this outdated operating system fails to meet the demands of the new work landscape, and its effectiveness has dwindled.

While the world of work experiences inertia and change takes time, we are reaching a tipping point where the limitations of Motivation 2.0 become increasingly evident. The COVID-19 pandemic has acted as a catalyst, sparking a rebellion against the status quo of work. People are seeking a better way to engage with their work, refusing to return to mundane and unfulfilling routines. A revolution is on the horizon, prompting an upgrade to the WorkOS.

Games offer a glimpse into the potential of engaging work experiences. They captivate us, immersing us in problem-solving and intense focus. Games tell us something profound about ourselves—we crave engagement, challenge, and accomplishment. Author Jane McGonigal explores these insights in her book, *Reality Is Broken: Why Games Make Us Better and How They Can Change the World.*[3] However, moderation is key, as excessive gaming can detract from personal relationships. Striking a balance with an average of three hours of gaming per day and 21 hours per week is considered ideal for maintaining a healthy engagement with games.

Interestingly, the three-to four-hour mark also emerges in unexpected realms. In the thought-provoking book, *Rest*, by Alex Soojung-Kim Pang,[4] the author reveals that four hours a day is the optimal time for deep, focused work. Renowned scientists throughout history have attested to the power of concentrated work sessions. However, the key lies in minimizing interruptions and distractions. By understanding the science of rest and focused work, we can harness our intrinsic motivations and achieve a state of flow, both in games and in our professional lives.

As the world shifts toward a new paradigm of work, the upgrade to our WorkOS becomes essential. By embracing the principles of intrinsic motivation, we can create more fulfilling and engaging work experiences that tap into our inherent drives and passions.

Motivation

When it comes to motivation, it's not just about external factors like rewards and incentives. The science of motivation delves into the intrinsic reasons that drive us to find meaning and fulfillment in our work. Intrinsic motivations, such as curiosity, creativity, and problem-solving, tap into our innate desires and make work more enjoyable and engaging.

Self-determination theory (SDT) provides valuable insights into human motivation and personality. It highlights the importance of three basic psychological needs: autonomy, competence, and relatedness. Autonomy refers to our natural inclination for self-direction and control over our lives. Competence involves feeling capable and effective in our actions and having opportunities for growth. Relatedness is our inclination to form positive relationships and contribute to the well-being of others.

Meeting these psychological needs is essential for intrinsic motivation. When we feel a sense of autonomy, competence, and relatedness in our work, we are more likely to be intrinsically motivated and engage in healthy, creative, and enjoyable behaviors. Supportive environments that foster autonomy, competence, and relatedness, along with strategies that promote well-being, contribute to the fulfillment of these needs.

SDT also distinguishes between autonomous and controlled motivation. Autonomous motivation arises from internal factors like interests and values, while controlled motivation stems from external factors like rewards and punishment. Internalizing these factors leads to more self-determined motivation, while externalizing them results in more controlled, extrinsic motivation.

SDT aligns with the concept of intrinsic motivation in games. Games offer autonomy through choice and control, competence through challenges and improvement opportunities, and relatedness through social connections. By satisfying these intrinsic needs, games become highly motivating to play.

In understanding the relationship between SDT and Maslow's Hierarchy of Needs, we find that they complement each other. Maslow's theory focuses on different levels of needs that must be met in a specific order, from physiological to self-actualization. SDT, on the other hand, emphasizes the innate psychological needs for autonomy, competence, and relatedness as the foundation of motivation and well-being. SDT explores the underlying psychological processes behind these needs.

Games tap into our intrinsic motivations by providing challenges and rewards that align with our desires to learn, achieve, create, and socialize. Whether it's customization options that stimulate our creativity, complex tasks that engage our problem-solving skills, or multiplayer features that fulfill our need for connection, games keep us engaged and motivated by resonating with our intrinsic motivations.

As we continue to explore the science of motivation and harness our intrinsic drives, we can create work environments that inspire and fulfill us, leading to greater satisfaction and productivity.

Intrinsic vs. extrinsic motivations

Intrinsic motivations are the internal drives and desires that motivate us to engage in activities for their own sake. These motivations include the enjoyment of the activity, the desire to learn, achieve, create, express ourselves, socialize, and experience a sense of accomplishment or satisfaction. Research by Harry Harlow and Edward Deci demonstrated that intrinsic motivation is more effective at driving performance compared to extrinsic motivation, which relies on external rewards or punishments. They found that when people are intrinsically motivated, they are more likely to continue the activity even without external rewards, whereas extrinsic rewards can undermine intrinsic motivation and decrease interest in the activity.

Deci, Koestner, and Ryan conducted a meta-analysis[5] that further explored the effects of extrinsic rewards on intrinsic motivation. Their findings showed that extrinsic rewards have a generally negative impact on intrinsic motivation, especially when the rewards are controlling in nature. Controlling rewards, such as those used to manipulate or coerce individuals, tend to undermine intrinsic motivation. However, non-controlling extrinsic rewards, such as informational rewards that provide feedback and recognition, can have a positive impact on intrinsic motivation by enhancing feelings of competence and relatedness.

It's important to recognize that motivations exist on a spectrum, and individuals may have a dominant motivation that is influenced by various factors and circumstances throughout their lives. Understanding the effects of intrinsic and extrinsic motivations can guide us to create environments that support and nurture intrinsic motivation, leading to greater engagement and satisfaction.

Notable works on this topic include the meta-analytic review by Deci, Koestner, and Ryan (1999) and the publications by Ryan and Deci (2017)[6] and Niemiec and Ryan (2009)[7] that delve into self-determination theory and its application to motivation and well-being in different contexts, including education. These works provide valuable insights into the psychological needs underlying intrinsic motivation and shed light on the importance of autonomy, competence, and relatedness in fostering motivation and personal growth.

Cultivating intrinsic motivation and understanding the delicate balance between intrinsic and extrinsic motivations can have a profound impact on our engagement, performance, and overall well-being.

Priming

In the world of video games, psychological priming plays a significant role in enhancing our experience and engagement. Game designers strategically use priming techniques to influence our behavior and cognition, making the gameplay more enjoyable and immersive. By exposing us to certain stimuli, such as visual cues, sounds, or even specific words, they can prime our minds to think in particular ways and evoke specific emotions or thoughts.

For example, imagine playing a thrilling action game where you're immersed in a virtual world filled with intense battles. The game designers might incorporate intense music, dynamic visuals, and fast-paced gameplay to prime your mind for excitement and heightened focus. As a result, you become more engaged, your adrenaline surges, and you feel a sense of thrill and exhilaration.

In addition to enhancing our emotional experience, games also tap into our intrinsic motivations through behavioral priming. By aligning game mechanics with our innate desires, games create an environment that activates our natural drive for challenge, skill development, and autonomy.

Video games often present us with challenges that gradually increase in difficulty, allowing us to improve our skills and abilities over time. This progression primes us to continually strive for improvement, as each success reinforces our intrinsic motivation to overcome challenges and master the game.

Moreover, games provide us with a sense of control and autonomy over our actions and decisions within the game world. This freedom to make choices and shape the outcome of the game aligns with our intrinsic desire to have some level of control over our environment. By priming our sense of autonomy, games empower us and make us feel more engaged and invested in the gameplay experience.

By understanding the power of psychological priming, game designers can craft experiences that tap into our intrinsic motivations and create an immersive and enjoyable journey. These techniques can be applied to other areas of life, including work, where behavioral priming can be used to activate employees' intrinsic motivations and make their work more enjoyable and fulfilling.

In essence, psychological priming is a powerful tool that game designers use to influence our behavior and enhance our engagement in games. Through visual, auditory, and conceptual cues, video games can prime our minds to experience emotions, think in certain ways, and tap into our intrinsic motivations. By leveraging priming techniques, games create an environment that captivates us, keeps us engaged, and satisfies our natural desires for challenge, skill development, and autonomy.

Punishment vs. reward: unraveling motivational complexities

In the intricate dance of motivation, the interplay between punishment and reward holds a captivating allure. Yet, amidst the complexity lies a question: Does intrinsic motivation truly drive us all, or do some individuals find their primary motivation in the allure of extrinsic rewards? As we explore the shades of gray in this motivational spectrum, we unravel fascinating insights that challenge our preconceived notions.

Daniel Pink introduces the notion of a Type X personality, a compelling archetype, fueled predominantly by extrinsic motivation. This revelation disrupts the notion of a universal intrinsic motivation and urges us to consider the diverse tapestry of motivations that shape individuals. The dichotomy of "mercenaries" and "missionaries" emerges, revealing the contrast between those driven by self-interest and those propelled by a greater purpose.

However, let us tread cautiously when categorizing and labeling individuals. The uniqueness of each person defies capture in rigid boxes, for we are ever-evolving and multifaceted beings. While these categories can serve as initial frameworks for understanding, they should be treated as mental shortcuts— guiding our exploration rather than defining our limits. Embracing the complexity allows us to observe the intricate interplay between behaviors, environments, and the individuals themselves, enabling them to unleash their full potential.

Within the realm of motivations, we encounter the eternal debate of punishment versus reward. The effectiveness of these approaches is not a one-size-fits-all enigma. While rewards tend to generate more positive behavioral outcomes, punishment can have its place in specific contexts, such as deterring unacceptable or dangerous behavior. It is crucial to consider the nuances and intricacies of each situation, tailoring our approach accordingly.

Timing and type play vital roles in the realm of rewards and punishment. Tangible rewards, like monetary incentives, may be effective in promoting certain behaviors, but they may fall short when fostering creativity or tackling complex challenges. In contrast, intangible rewards, such as recognition and praise, tap into our social nature and intrinsic need for validation, igniting a deeper sense of motivation.

The essence of immediate reinforcement reveals itself as a potent catalyst for behavioral change. Delivering rewards or punishment promptly after the desired behavior strengthens the link between action and consequence, reinforcing the desired pattern. Delaying consequences can dilute their impact, as individuals may struggle to connect their actions with the rewards or punishment they receive, potentially perceiving the system as capricious or unjust.

Yet, beyond the realm of work and gamified experiences, we are drawn to the core essence of motivation—problem-solving and meaningful challenges. Games, in their purest form, epitomize this essence. However, the removal of problem-solving from a game transforms it into a mere activity, devoid of its captivating allure.

By infusing work with engaging and meaningful challenges, we tap into individuals' intrinsic motivations, fostering a profound sense of purpose and accomplishment.

Notes

1. Mihaly Csikszentmihalyi, *Flow: The Psychology of Optimal Experience* (New York: HarperCollins, 2009).
2. Daniel Pink, *Drive: The Surprising Truth About What Motivates Us* (Edinburgh: Canongate Books, 2011).
3. Jane McGonigal, *Reality Is Broken: Why Games Make Us Better and How They Can Change the World* (New York: Vintage, 2012).
4. Alex Soojung-Kim Pang, *Rest* (New York: Basic Books, 2016).
5. E.L., Deci, R. Koestner, and R.M. Ryan, A meta-analytic review of experiments examining the effects of extrinsic rewards on intrinsic motivation. *Psychological Bulletin*, 125(6) (1999): 627–668.
6. R.M. Ryan and E.L. Deci, *Self-Determination Theory: Basic Psychological Needs in Motivation, Development, and Wellness* (New York: Guilford Press, 2017).
7. C.P. Niemiec and R.M. Ryan, Autonomy, competence, and relatedness in the classroom: Applying self-determination theory to educational practice. *Theory and Research in Education*, 7(2) (2009): 133–144.

CHAPTER 10
FORCED MINDFULNESS: WHY IT REMOVES THE POWER OF FREEDOM AND CHOICE IN ENJOYMENT

From an early age, societal expectations and practicality often shape our aspirations. The innocent dreams of becoming an astronaut or a policeman are nudged toward more "practical" professions like lawyers, doctors, or computer engineers. Throughout our educational journey, the interplay of perceived desires, natural inclinations, and biases further muddles the path we choose to follow.

When it comes to games in the workplace, a common reaction is skepticism. We've witnessed misapplied attempts at gamification, usually centered around leaderboards and a one-size-fits-all approach. Yet, I understand and share your aversion. But, fear not, for there is a different path—one that truly works. Before delving into that, let's explore why previous gamification efforts fell short.

It's crucial to acknowledge that the problem lies not in games themselves but in the misguided implementation of gamification. Two key factors contribute to the futility of many gamification endeavors. First, not all work tasks are naturally suited for gamification. Forcing a game-like structure onto unengaging tasks can diminish both enjoyment and effectiveness. Second, gamification can be perceived as manipulative or condescending, implying that workers need external incentives or trickery to perform their duties. This erodes trust and breeds resentment between employees and management. Moreover, implementing gamification can be resource-intensive without guaranteeing improved performance or satisfaction.

Now, let me share a brief tale of forced mindfulness—a transformative experience that taught me the value of individuality.

In a bustling London conference room, young managers gathered for a leadership development program. To our surprise, we found ourselves participating in guided meditation. While some closed their eyes, a lingering discomfort compelled me to keep mine wide open.

This forced mindfulness encounter was a vivid reminder that a one-size-fits-all approach fails to resonate with everyone. Assuming that what works for one person will work for all is a flawed premise, alienating those who do not naturally resonate with a particular approach. Our brains, wired with a bias toward familiarity, seek solace in the familiar faces and experiences that once ensured our tribe's survival. However, as the world expands, this assumption becomes a trap, hindering our ability to adapt and understand the diverse needs of individuals.

The lessons from forced mindfulness highlight the negative effects of coercion. When we feel compelled or forced into an activity, it breeds apathy and tension, even if the intention was to create a sense of fun. Consider being coerced into attending an amusement park for a company team-building activity—it quickly loses its luster compared to freely choosing to go. This intriguing observation points us toward a crucial element of enjoyment: the association with freedom and choice.

When we have the freedom to choose, when we feel empowered to decide our path, fun becomes an organic expression of our intrinsic motivations. It aligns with our unique preferences and ignites a genuine sense of enjoyment. Embracing this concept unlocks a world of possibilities in fostering an engaging work environment—one that respects individuality and offers autonomy in how tasks are approached.

In the realm of gamification, let us embrace the power of freedom and choice. By designing work experiences that honor individual preferences and allow employees to find their unique paths, we tap into intrinsic motivations that drive genuine enjoyment and fulfillment. Just as forced mindfulness fails to capture the essence of true mindfulness, forced fun hampers the authentic sense of pleasure that emerges when individuals have the freedom to embrace activities that align with their own desires.

So, as we navigate the intricacies of motivation and seek to create a vibrant work environment, remember the transformative impact of freedom and choice. By unlocking the potential within each individual and fostering a sense of autonomy, we pave the way for a truly engaging, enjoyable, and purpose-driven workplace.

The nature of active engagement and intrinsic motivation

In exploring the distinction between passive entertainment, such as watching Netflix or TikTok, and active engagement in video games, we find a fundamental difference—the pattern of consumption. Both forms of entertainment provide choices, but games tap into an active problem-solving pattern, while platforms like Netflix appeal to our innate love for storytelling.

Our brains are wired for learning, as evidenced by the existence of a built-in rewards center that releases dopamine—the "feel-good hormone"—whenever we engage in activities that enhance our chances of survival. Long before the invention of books, information was transmitted through stories. Those who patiently listened and absorbed these stories gained valuable knowledge about the savanna's hidden lion, sources of food, or the art of building a fire. Over generations, our brains learned to reward us for this behavior. Play and games fell into the realm of active learning, a vital component for our survival. They allowed us to hone our physical and mental skills without the immediate risks present in the wild.

Even in today's concrete jungle, our ancestral machinery remains intact. Recognizing its nature and harnessing its potential to tackle modern challenges are crucial. Games have always played a significant role in our survival, serving as a means to practice essential skills in a safe and engaging manner. This intrinsic draw to games underscores their importance throughout human history and persists to this day.

Harnessing the power of OKRs and meaningful goals

OKRs, or Objectives and Key Results, have emerged as a powerful management tool utilized by prominent companies like Google and various unicorn startups worldwide. What makes OKRs so powerful, and should they be a part of the WorkOS 2.0 arsenal?

Originally stemming from the concept of management by objectives introduced by management guru, Peter Drucker, OKRs were refined and popularized by Andy Grove during his tenure as CEO at Intel. Grove recognized the need to incorporate measurable results into the equation, especially in the rapidly evolving landscape of advanced computer components that Intel navigated. This tool proved to be a better fit for the emerging generation of knowledge-based companies.

John Doerr, who was part of Intel's management team and later became a legendary venture capitalist, introduced OKRs to the portfolio companies at Kleiner Perkins Caufield & Byers, a renowned player in the global internet revolution. One such portfolio company was a small startup founded by Stanford PhD students—Google.

The founders of Google enthusiastically embraced OKRs as a management tool, and it played a pivotal role in the exponential growth and innovation that Google has achieved over the years. Larry Page, CEO of Alphabet, credits OKRs for helping the company achieve 10x growth and staying on track with their audacious mission of organizing the world's information.

The true magic lies in making progress visible and shortening the feedback cycle. Rather than relying on the traditional one-year retrospective reviews, companies like Google have adopted a more agile approach, reviewing progress on a monthly or even weekly basis. This accelerated feedback loop propels both companies and individuals forward, boosting their velocity and driving them to new levels of success.

However, it is important to recognize that setting the right goals is just one piece of the game. John Doerr emphasizes the significance of setting meaningful and audacious goals, but execution is what truly matters. The simplicity of the goal-setting system is key—knowing what needs to be accomplished and how to achieve it. Many of us often set goals without a clear sense of purpose, lacking a compelling "why" behind them.

In the words of Confucius, "Our greatest glory is not in never falling, but in rising every time we fall." OKRs provide the framework and visibility to learn from failures, adapt, and continue rising toward our aspirations. By harnessing the power of meaningful goals, coupled with effective execution, organizations can unlock their full potential and achieve remarkable outcomes in the dynamic landscape of the WorkOS 2.0.

Embracing funny failure in games and work

Failure is often seen as a dreaded concept in the workplace, associated with negative connotations like pain, screw-ups, and career-limiting moves. The prevailing corporate culture encourages individuals to avoid failure at all costs, creating an environment where gossiping about others' failures becomes the norm. However, when it comes to games, failure takes on an entirely different meaning.

In games, failure is not only acceptable but also an essential part of the experience. Without the downs, players wouldn't appreciate the ups, resulting in a flat and uninteresting game. Video game designers understand this and incorporate various techniques to make failure enjoyable and a valuable learning tool.

One approach is injecting humor into failure. By including silly animations, jokes, or exaggerated responses, games transform the experience into a more light-hearted and enjoyable one. Laughter can ease the sting of failure and encourage players to persevere.

Another strategy is turning failure into a valuable learning opportunity. Games often provide players with insights, tips, or tutorials on how to improve their performance. This transforms failure into a stepping stone toward mastery, making players feel like they are progressing and getting better with each setback.

The idea of progress and moving forward, even in the face of failure, is another aspect that makes the game experience enjoyable. Games typically employ reward systems that incentivize players to continue trying, offering a sense of achievement when they overcome obstacles and make progress.

Breaking the game up into short, manageable sessions is another way to make failure more enjoyable. By allowing players to easily pick up where they left off, video games minimize the daunting feeling of failure and encourage repeated attempts.

The competitive aspect of games can also enhance the enjoyment of failure. When players can compare their scores and progress with others, a sense of community and camaraderie is fostered. Failure becomes a shared experience, and the drive to improve and outperform others adds excitement and motivation.

Lastly, striking the right balance between challenge and attainability is crucial. Games should be challenging enough to keep players engaged, but not so difficult that failure becomes discouraging. Overcoming a difficult obstacle after repeated failures is immensely rewarding, further enhancing the enjoyment of the game.

These lessons from games can be applied to the workplace, encouraging a more positive and growth-oriented approach to failure. By embracing the idea that failure is an opportunity for learning and improvement, individuals and organizations can foster a culture that encourages innovation, resilience, and continuous growth.

Summary

This chapter explores a few key flaws of forced gamification. We found out why many attempts at gamification in the workplace fail due to forced implementation and a one-size-fits-all approach. We discovered that it generally leads to employee dissatisfaction, short-term lack of engagement, and long-term loss of trust.

The power of freedom and choice emphasizes the significance of allowing employees to choose their path, aligning with their intrinsic motivations, to foster a more enjoyable and productive work environment.

We differentiated between active engagement in games and passive entertainment like watching Netflix. Games tap into a rewarding pattern of active problem-solving, while passive forms cater to our love for storytelling.

We then found out why Objectives and Key Results (OKRs) are an effective management tool that aligns goals with measurable outcomes, as shown in companies like Google.

Finally, we found out that approaching failure in a positive way helps us use lessons from game design to make failure a source of learning and growth.

PART IV
THE INTERSECTION BETWEEN GAMES AND WORK

CHAPTER 11
HOW WE LEARN

By recognizing the intersection between games and work, we can tap into the inherent motivation and enjoyment that games provide and apply it to our work experiences. Rather than viewing work as a mundane or tedious task, we can strive to make it more engaging, fulfilling, and even fun. This requires a shift in mindset, where we embrace the idea that work can be enjoyable and that our natural drive and curiosity can be harnessed to enhance our productivity and satisfaction.

Education systems have traditionally focused on a one-size-fits-all approach, where students are expected to conform to rigid structures and predetermined goals. This approach often suppresses individuality and intrinsic motivation, limiting the potential for creativity and passion in learning. However, by incorporating elements of game-like experiences into education, we can create a more engaging and effective learning environment. Games have the power to ignite curiosity, promote problem-solving, and provide immediate feedback, all of which can enhance the learning process.

Applying the principles of games to work can have a transformative effect on our productivity and overall satisfaction. By introducing elements of challenge, autonomy, and rewards, we can create a work environment that aligns with our intrinsic motivations and fosters a sense of purpose and accomplishment. This may involve setting meaningful goals, providing opportunities for skill development and growth, and encouraging collaboration and healthy competition among team members.

In the intersection between games and work, we have the opportunity to redefine our approach to work and unlock our full potential. By embracing the principles of games and integrating them into our work experiences, we can create a more engaging, enjoyable, and ultimately more successful professional journey.

Free schools

In our exploration of the intersection between games and work, it is important to examine how we learn and the role of alternative educational models in fostering intrinsic motivation and a love of learning. One such model is the concept of free schools, which prioritize creativity, self-directed learning, and play.

Free schools operate on the belief that children learn best when they are motivated by their own interests and desires. Instead of relying on external rewards or punishments, students are encouraged to pursue their passions through hands-on activities, games, and play. Teachers act as facilitators, supporting and guiding students as they explore their own learning paths. This approach aims to nurture critical thinking, creativity, and a lifelong love of learning.

The roots of free schools can be traced back to the progressive education movement of the late nineteenth and early twentieth centuries, championed by figures like John Dewey and Jean Piaget. These pioneers advocated for student-centered, experiential learning that focused on active engagement and autonomy.

Studies have shown that students in free schools exhibit higher levels of motivation and engagement compared to their peers in traditional schools. However, it is important to acknowledge that the self-directed approach may not be suitable for everyone. Some students may require the extrinsic motivation of grades to stay motivated and engaged in their learning journey.

Free schools are not the only alternative educational models that emphasize learning through play and games. The Montessori Method, the Reggio Emilia Approach, and Waldorf Education are other examples of child-centered approaches that recognize the value of hands-on, imaginative learning experiences.

These educational approaches align with the idea that games and play have a profound impact on learning and motivation. They create environments where students can explore, experiment, and discover at their own pace, fostering a sense of curiosity and intrinsic motivation.

Challenging the dichotomy

Halliday: I created the Oasis because I never felt at home in the real world. I just didn't know how to connect with people there. I was afraid for all my life, right up until the day I knew my life was ending. And that was when I realized that . . . as terrifying and painful as reality can be, it's also . . . the only place that . . . you can get a decent meal. Because, reality . . . is real.

Parzival: People come to the Oasis for all the things they can do, but they stay for all the things they can be.

Imagine a world where work and play merge seamlessly, where the boundaries between the two blur and our innate curiosity and love for learning take center stage. In the realm of the video game, Ready Player One, Halliday, the creator of the Oasis, reflects on his creation and the stark contrast he felt between the real world and the virtual realm. But as he faces the end of his life, he realizes that, despite its challenges, reality is where true sustenance lies.

Now, make this wisdom the intersection between games and work. Traditionally, work has been seen as a necessary evil, a means to an end, while play has been reserved for leisure and escape. But what if we challenged this dichotomy? What if we discovered that work and play aren't as different as we once believed?

Enter the world of free schools and alternative education, where the spirit of play and self-directed learning reigns supreme. These innovative models recognize that true learning happens when we are motivated by our own passions and interests, not by external rewards or punishments. In these schools, students embrace creativity, critical thinking, and hands-on exploration, guided by teachers who act as facilitators rather than dictators.

Yet, we must acknowledge that not everyone thrives solely on intrinsic motivation. Just as in the vast landscape of games, where players have different preferences and playstyles, individuals in the realm of education and work also possess diverse motivational profiles. Some may require external incentives or measurable outcomes to stay engaged and motivated. Recognizing and catering to these differences are key to creating inclusive and effective learning and work environments.

So, how do we harness the power of play and intrinsic motivation in the realm of work? It starts with understanding our own game personalities, uncovering the games that sparked our passions during our formative years. By aligning our work with our natural inclinations, we unlock a world of joy and fulfillment. Simultaneously, we must reevaluate how work is classified and assigned, ensuring that tasks align with the motivations and strengths of individuals.

If you were immersed for hours in a racing game like Need for Speed and loved competing against others, you would find the thrill of achieving sales targets naturally motivating. Similarly, if an individual gravitates to strategy games like Sid Meier's Civilization, they will discover marketing is a much better match with their natural inclinations.

But don't forget the importance of autonomy and choice. Just as players can switch games to suit their preferences, we should have the flexibility to switch work domains, keeping ourselves engaged and invigorated. The notion of quitting, often stigmatized in the workplace, can actually be a catalyst for personal growth and renewed purpose.

In her insightful book, *Quit*,[1] author Annie Duke describes how we often wait to quit too late and lose out on the opportunities that might be right in front of us due to the natural tendency for loss aversion. The most challenging thing is to get the timing right and balance quitting with grit. Quit too early, and you lose out on many learning opportunities and trust equity, but quit too late, and you risk stagnating and getting stuck in the wrong work. Another author who taught me to think better about quitting is Reid Hoffman, the co-founder of LinkedIn, who wrote an incredibly insightful book. In his book, *The Alliance: Managing Talent in the Networked Age,*[2] he described the tour of duty that equals two years and starts with an explicit commitment from an individual and their work leader. I found this concept extremely useful and have often used it for myself and those working with me.

Priming Work

Now we look once more at the concept of priming (see Chapter 9), where subtle cues shape our perceptions and behaviors. By infusing work environments with positive associations, we can transform mundane tasks into engaging experiences. Just as video games captivate us with their immersive worlds and enjoyable challenges, we can infuse work with elements of excitement, meaning, and a sense of progress.

The design of Airbnb's meeting rooms resembles actual units listed on their platform. This immersive environment serves as a constant reminder of the customer experience and primes employees to think from the user's perspective. It's a subtle way to foster empathy and alignment with their mission to create unique travel experiences.

On the surface, Google's work environments look like cool startup offices with bright, open layouts, with playful furnishings. But these elements promote creativity, collaboration, and well-being below the fun surface, subtly priming employees for innovation.

Apple built its new headquarters, designing it with aesthetics, functionality, and purpose. The open floor plan and common areas foster collaboration and serendipitous employee encounters. The use of glass and the seamless integration of indoor and outdoor spaces serve as a subtle priming for careful design and interconnected thinking.

And what about the brave souls who venture into the realm of game design? Their journey is a testament to the power of passion and autonomy. While financial rewards may not always be extravagant, the intrinsic joy of creating and shaping interactive experiences is their driving force. It reminds us that work can be a creative endeavor, a realm where we sculpt meaningful contributions and find purpose beyond monetary gains.

As we unravel the intersection between games and work, we realize that the lines that once divided them are fading. We have the power to redefine our approach to work, to create environments where play, curiosity, and genuine enjoyment are celebrated.

Infinite games

Imagine a game without an end, a game where the goal is not to win or reach a conclusion, but to keep the play going indefinitely. These are the realms of infinite games, a concept introduced by philosopher James P. Carse in his book, *Finite and Infinite Games*.[3]

Infinite games are in stark contrast to the finite games we typically encounter. While finite games have a clear objective and a definitive endpoint, infinite games are all about continuous play and engagement. The purpose is not to win, but to keep the game alive and to embrace the joy of participating.

Carse's book explores the fundamental distinction between finite and infinite games and shows how this distinction applies not only to games themselves but also to our lives and interactions. He suggests that understanding this difference is crucial in shaping our worldview and our relationships with others.

When we view our work through the lens of an infinite game, a profound shift occurs. Instead of obsessing over winning or achieving specific goals, we shift our focus to continuous growth, learning, and building relationships in our daily work. Work becomes an ongoing journey of exploration and collaboration, where the process itself holds more value than any final outcome.

In the infinite game of work, success is not measured by reaching a fixed endpoint. It is measured by the quality of our engagement, the relationships we forge, and the ongoing improvement we experience. This perspective encourages us to prioritize learning, adaptability, and the development of a supportive and collaborative work community.

By embracing the principles of the infinite game, work takes on a new meaning. It becomes a source of fulfillment and purpose, free from the pressures and constraints of finite games. We no longer seek to reach an endpoint but rather revel in the never-ending process of growth, learning, and meaningful engagement.

So let us change our mindset and embrace the infinite game of work, where each day becomes an opportunity to play, learn, and connect with others. In this realm, the possibilities are endless, and the rewards lie not in winning, but in the pleasure of the work itself.

Applying game development principles to work

The process of creating a game shares many similarities with the challenges we encounter in the workplace. By applying game development principles to our work, we can enhance our productivity, engagement, and overall satisfaction. These principles can be translated to the context of work:

1. **Define the goal of your work:** Just as a game needs a clear objective, it's essential to define the goals of your work. Understand what you want to achieve and what success looks like for your projects or tasks. Clear goals provide direction and a sense of purpose, allowing you to stay focused and motivated.

2. **Develop effective work mechanics:** Work mechanics refer to the systems and processes that govern how you approach and complete your tasks. Design workflows and strategies that optimize efficiency, streamline communication, and promote collaboration. By developing effective work mechanics, you can enhance productivity and ensure smooth progress toward your work goals.

3. **Prototype and iterate on your work methods:** Similar to building a video game prototype, don't be afraid to

experiment and iterate on your work methods. Test different approaches, tools, and techniques to find what works best for you and your team. Continuously refine and improve your work processes based on feedback and data-driven insights.

4. **Design engaging work environments:** Just as video game assets create a visually appealing and immersive experience, design your work environment to be engaging and stimulating. Create a workspace that promotes creativity, collaboration, and a positive mindset. Incorporate elements that inspire and motivate you, such as personalized decor, natural lighting, or inspiring quotes on the notice-board.

5. **Develop your skills and knowledge:** Game development involves continuous learning and skill development. Apply the same mindset to your work by seeking opportunities to grow and expand your expertise. Invest time in continuing professional development (CPD), attend workshops or conferences, and actively seek 360° feedback to improve your skills.

6. **Playtest and gather feedback:** In video game development, playtesting and gathering feedback are crucial for refining the game experience. Similarly, seek 360° feedback from colleagues, supervisors, or mentors on your work. Embrace constructive criticism and use it as an opportunity to identify areas for improvement and growth. Continuous feedback loops can lead to enhanced performance and greater job satisfaction.

By applying video game development principles in our work, we can transform our professional lives into engaging and rewarding experiences. Embracing a goal-oriented mindset, optimizing work mechanics, creating stimulating environments, and embracing continuous professional learning and 360° feedback can significantly enhance our productivity, motivation, and overall success in the workplace. So, bring the spirit of video game development into your work and unlock your full potential.

Summary

In this chapter, we explored the unique nature of games and their significance in human culture throughout history. Games have been a part of our lives for thousands of years and have a remarkable ability to fulfill our wishes and immerse us in captivating experiences.

Games have a distinct quality that sets them apart from other forms of entertainment. They provide us with a sense of agency, challenge, and achievement, allowing us to actively participate and shape the outcome of the experience. Whether it's conquering a virtual world, solving puzzles, or competing with others, games have a way of captivating our attention and sparking our imagination.

One interesting concept explored here is priming, which involves using previous experiences to influence our thoughts and behaviors in the present moment. By associating work with positive experiences or concepts, we can create a more engaging and enjoyable work environment. Priming can help change our mindset from viewing work as a tedious chore to seeing it as an opportunity for growth, creativity, and collaboration.

Throughout this journey, we discovered the intersection between games and work and found that the principles of video game development can be applied to our professional lives, leading to increased productivity, engagement, and satisfaction. By defining clear goals, developing effective work mechanics, creating engaging environments, and embracing continuous professional learning and 360° feedback, we can transform our work experience into a fulfilling and meaningful endeavor.

Notes

1. Annie Duke, *Quit: The Power of Knowing When to Walk Away* (New York: Penguin Publishing Group, 2022).
2. Reid Hoffman, Ben Casnocha, and Chris Yeh, *The Alliance: Managing Talent in the Networked Age* (Boston: Harvard Business Review Press, 2014).
3. James P. Carse, Finite and *Infinite Games* (New York: Free Press, 2023).

CHAPTER 12
EMBRACING OPEN SOURCE: UNLEASHING THE POWER OF COLLABORATION

Imagine a world where software development is driven not by profit margins or corporate agendas, but by a global community of passionate individuals working together to create innovative solutions. This is the world of open source, where the boundaries of traditional work are shattered, and the possibilities are endless.

We now delve into the fascinating realm of open source software, a collaborative movement that challenges the notion of paid work as the sole driver of productivity. Surprisingly, it turns out that around 90% of all software in the world is developed by individuals who are not financially compensated for their efforts. This stark contrast to the traditional work model begs the question: how can people be motivated to contribute their time and expertise without the allure of monetary rewards or KPIs?

Open source software is a revolution in the tech industry, offering a refreshing alternative to proprietary software. Its core principle is simple yet profound: the source code is made freely available to the public, allowing anyone to view, modify, and distribute it. This openness unleashes a torrent of creativity, as individuals from diverse backgrounds and locations collaborate to improve and expand upon the software.

What drives this global army of volunteers to dedicate their time and energy to open source projects? The answer lies in intrinsic motivation—the internal desire to engage in an activity because it is inherently enjoyable, interesting, or fulfilling. Open source projects tap into the deep well of intrinsic motivation by offering a playground for learning, exploration, and problem-solving. Contributors are drawn to the technology itself, the challenge of solving complex problems, and the vibrant communities that form around these projects.

The recruitment of contributors in open source projects is a fascinating process. Online platforms like GitHub, Stack Overflow, and Reddit serve as bustling marketplaces, where projects advertise opportunities and potential contributors showcase their skills. Conferences and events provide invaluable networking opportunities, where developers can forge connections, share ideas, and ignite collaborations. The allure of open source development is not just the chance to work on cutting-edge projects, but also to be part of a vibrant community, exchanging knowledge, support, and camaraderie.

But how do open source projects ensure the quality and reliability of the software when there are no financial incentives or managerial hierarchies? The secret lies in the power of the community itself. Dedicated teams of core contributors, often experienced and respected members of the community, review and merge contributions from others. Their deep understanding of the project's goals and standards ensures that only high-quality code makes its way into the software. Detailed guidelines, coding standards, and review processes provide a roadmap for contributors, fostering a culture of excellence and continuous improvement.

One captivating tale that showcases the transformative impact of open source is the story of Linus Torvalds, the mastermind behind the Linux operating system. Torvalds single-handedly disrupted the world of closed-source operating systems by creating an open source alternative. His vision empowered developers worldwide to contribute their expertise, resulting in the widespread adoption of Linux and its derivatives. The success of Linux demonstrates the immense power of collaboration and community-driven development.

Open source and work

Open source software is not just a playground for tech enthusiasts—it has profound implications for the future of work. By embracing the principles of open source, we challenge the traditional notion that work is solely driven by extrinsic rewards, i.e., money. Instead, open source invites us to reimagine work as a realm of self-motivated exploration, growth, and collective achievement. It encourages a mindset shift from competition to collaboration, from fixed goals to continuous learning, and from individual achievements to the collective pursuit of excellence.

By adopting open source principles in our own work environments, we can unlock our untapped potential and foster a culture of creativity, autonomy, and purpose. Imagine the impact if organizations empowered their employees to contribute to open source projects at work, aligned with their interests and expertise. The sense of fulfillment, the development of new skills, and the rich connections formed within the global open source community would transcend the limitations of traditional work.

A community of engaged contributors works together to build open source projects to create something better than anything anyone could produce alone. This collaboration model can create more innovative and efficient work teams by engaging a mix of on-demand freelance communities and partner organizations working or interested in a particular project.

As we wrap up this chapter, open source software development stands as a testament to the power of collaboration, intrinsic motivation, and shared goals. By embracing open source principles, we can reshape the future of work, transcending the boundaries of profit-driven endeavors and embracing a world where collective passion and expertise fuel innovation. The possibilities are limitless, and the rewards are not just financial but also intellectual, emotional, and communal.

The source code behind the open source projects is freely available for anyone to see, modify, and build upon. This radical transparency allows for the deduplication of efforts and improves the quality of the end product. Applying it to work would mean that many of the work products can be made freely available, for example, rather than each insurance company developing their proprietary policies, they would create a version that they would make available for all the other insurance companies to collaborate and improve, as long as they keep it open and transparent too. This could create new, more straightforward, and better insurance.

NVIDIA, an American multinational technology company and world leader in AI computing, stands at the forefront of applying the open source approach to work. The organization embodies the spirit of collaboration and innovation by supporting and actively contributing to various open source initiatives, such as the NVIDIA Deep Learning Software Development Kit, that is openly and freely shared. The commitment to transparency, seen in sharing valuable research and tools with the broader software developer community, resonates with the open source philosophy of openness and shared growth. NVIDIA's provision of educational resources, such as free workshops and tutorials, aligns with the intrinsic motivations that drive open source contributors, fostering a culture of continuous learning and inclusivity.

CHAPTER 13
ESPORTS WORK: BLURRING THE LINES BETWEEN PLAY AND PROFESSION

In the immersive world of esports or electronic sports, work takes on a whole new meaning. This is a realm where the boundaries between play and profession become indistinguishable, and where the pursuit of mastery and competition intertwine. Wade, the protagonist in the video game, Ready Player One, found solace and purpose in the Oasis, dedicating his life to gaming. While his story may be fictional, it resonates with the millions of esports enthusiasts who have made gaming their livelihood.

Esports is a rapidly growing industry that centers around competitive video gaming. With over three billion players worldwide, esports has transcended the realm of casual entertainment and has become a highly organized and professionalized field. What sets esports apart is the level of dedication and passion that players bring to their craft, treating it not just as a hobby, but as a full-time career.

The rise of esports can be attributed to the convergence of technological advances, widespread internet connectivity, and the insatiable appetite for competitive gaming. The history of esports can be traced back to the emergence of video game competitions in the 1970s and 1980s, where gamers would gather in video arcades to test their skills. As technology progressed and online gaming became more prevalent, esports began to gain mainstream recognition.

One of the most interesting stories in the world of esports is that of Lee Sang-hyeok, known by his gaming alias "Faker." Widely regarded as the greatest League of Legends player of all time, Faker's journey showcases the immense dedication and passion that esports professionals bring to their work.

Starting at a young age, Faker honed his skills in League of Legends, eventually joining the Korean esports team SK Telecom T1. His exceptional talent and unwavering commitment have won him numerous championships and earned him global recognition. Faker's story highlights the transformative power of pursuing work that aligns with one's passion and interests, making it not just a job, but a source of deep fulfillment.

Esports work requires a unique set of skills and attributes. The reaction time of esports professionals is astonishingly fast, as they need to rapidly process and respond to complex visual stimuli within the game in seconds. Studies have shown that esports players often exhibit faster reaction times than professional athletes in traditional sports. This heightened ability to react quickly and make split-second decisions sets the stage for intense competition and strategic gameplay.

What sets esports apart from traditional sports is the ability to quickly quantify and analyze performance data. Actions per second (APS) is a metric used to measure player speed and efficiency. While an average casual player may have a range of 1–3 APS, professional esports players can achieve a staggering 10 APS. This level of skill requires immense concentration, control, and lightning-fast reaction times. It's a testament to the dedication and training that esports professionals undergo to excel in their chosen games.

How esports relate to the world of work

Esports work provides an intriguing perspective on the intersection of play and profession. Players often transition between different games, based on their preferences and the demands of the audience. This flexibility and autonomy in choosing their gaming endeavors keep the passion alive and prevent the burnout often associated with traditional jobs. Most esports professionals genuinely enjoy what they do, as they have invested countless hours mastering their craft and becoming skilled in their chosen games. Imagine if you could apply this flexibility to learn, practice, fail, and master other types of work on your own terms.

The transferable skills gained in esports are also noteworthy. Strategizing, teamwork, and adaptability acquired in one game can be carried over to other games, making esports work a continuous journey of growth and learning. Much like traditional professional development, esports offers opportunities for players to showcase their skills, earn recognition, and progress in their careers.

The success of esports games hinges on three crucial elements. First, watchability plays a vital role in captivating audiences. Games that are easy to follow and understand for casual viewers make for an engaging spectator experience. Second, skill-based gameplay ensures that advanced skills translate to a clear advantage in the game. This skill gap adds excitement and tension to matches, as the outcome is not always predictable. Finally, the element of chance introduces unpredictability and keeps the games thrilling, as even the most skilled players are not guaranteed victory. The combination of these elements makes esports competitions a thrilling spectacle for fans worldwide.

Drawing inspiration from the world of esports, we can explore ways to infuse more choice and autonomy into traditional work environments. Instead of always assigning the same tasks to the same people, randomizing work tasks from time to time can help to keep things fresh and interesting, and it can also help to develop employees' skills in different areas.

Moreover, embracing chance at work means recognizing that there are many uncontrollable factors, especially in more difficult problems and innovative things that have not been done before.

Allowing employees to have more control over their tasks, projects, and schedules enhances their sense of ownership and motivation. Providing regular feedback and support empowers employees to take charge of their work and drive their success. Emphasizing continuous professional learning and skill development creates an environment where work becomes a fulfilling and engaging journey.

The concept of "flow" is often mentioned in the context of work, referring to the state of being fully absorbed and immersed in an activity (see Chapter 9). In esports, players experience this flow as they become completely engrossed in their gameplay, losing track of time and feeling a deep sense of fulfillment.

Esports work challenges conventional notions of work by demonstrating that it can be an immersive and deeply satisfying experience. The ability to quantify and analyze performance data provides a unique perspective on skill development and progression, offering valuable insights into players' strengths and areas for improvement.

Summary

In the world of esports, the line between games and work blurs as players dedicate themselves to becoming professionals in competitive video gaming. With the ability to achieve lightning-fast reaction times, esports professionals showcase the immense concentration and control required to excel in their chosen games. While close to 10 actions per second may seem superhuman, the dedication and passion that these players bring to their work make it an incredibly engaging and rewarding experience.

Esports work challenges the conventional notion of what work means. It demonstrates that work can be an immersive and meaningful experience when fueled by passion, dedication, and the pursuit of excellence. As esports continues to grow and evolve, it serves as a reminder that the boundaries between work and play are fluid, and that finding work worth doing can truly be the greatest prize in life.

The intersection of games and work in esports opens up new possibilities for creating a more engaging, rewarding, and meaningful work environment. By embracing the dedication and passion exhibited in esports, we can reshape our understanding of work, allowing individuals to pursue their passions, develop their skills, and find fulfillment in their professional endeavors.

Drawing inspiration from the world of esports, we can reimagine work as an immersive and fulfilling endeavor. By infusing elements of choice, autonomy, skill development, and passion, we can transform work into a realm where individuals feel deeply engaged, motivated, and rewarded.

PART V
LEVEL-UP WORK

CHAPTER 14
LEVEL 1 SKILLS: BREAKING FREE FROM THE SKILLS TRAP

It's time to break free from the limiting view that equates a person's worth solely with their collection of skills, driven by financial incentives. While this perspective served its purpose during the era of skilled factory workers operating complex machinery, we must now embrace a broader understanding of human potential in the age of the internet and knowledge economy.

In the rapidly evolving landscape of the post-knowledge economy, where knowledge and intelligence are being democratized through advances in technology, focusing solely on skills neglects crucial factors such as drive, motivations, work style, values, and culture. These elements significantly impact job performance and satisfaction, highlighting the need for a more holistic approach.

While skills are undoubtedly important, they are not the ultimate predictor of job success. They serve as a rough tool that we have relied upon due to their tangibility. However, in a fast-changing world, some skills can quickly become obsolete. Relying solely on skills-based matching may lead to a mismatch between a candidate's skills and the evolving requirements of the job, resulting in reduced productivity and dissatisfaction.

Furthermore, the process of assessing skills can be subject to bias, whether conscious or unconscious. Bias in skill assessment can lead to certain candidates being overlooked or unfairly excluded from consideration, depriving organizations of valuable talent and diversity.

Focusing exclusively on a candidate's existing skills also hinders our ability to recognize their potential for growth and development. A candidate who may now not possess all the required skills for a specific role can still be a strong candidate if they demonstrate a willingness to learn and possess a growth mindset. By overlooking the potential for growth, we miss out on individuals who can bring fresh perspectives, adaptability, and a hunger for continuous improvement.

To navigate this changing landscape effectively, we must expand our evaluation criteria beyond skills alone. We need to consider a candidate's intrinsic motivations, values alignment, cultural fit, and their ability to embrace change and learn new skills. By embracing a more holistic approach to assessing individuals, we can unlock untapped potential and build diverse, high-performing teams that thrive in a dynamic and uncertain world.

As we venture into the future of work, it is imperative to recognize that skills are just one piece of the puzzle. We must embrace a paradigm shift that values individual potential, adaptability, and the drive to continually learn and grow. By breaking free from the skill trap, we open ourselves up to a world of possibilities and create an environment where individuals can truly thrive.

What is a better predictor of success when matching people to work?

By categorizing and understanding the compatibility between game types and specific work contexts, we can unlock the potential within individuals and facilitate the creation of harmonious and rewarding career paths. Embracing the multifaceted nature of human inclinations cultivates a workforce that thrives on their unique strengths, leading to increased engagement, fulfillment, and success in the dynamic landscape of work.

There are four distinct player types, each with their own dynamic fit within the realm of work: Achievers, Explorers, Socializers, and Challengers. See also Chapter 8.

- **Achievers**, the champions of goal-oriented endeavors. They thrive in work environments that offer clear objectives, measurable outcomes, and opportunities for growth and recognition. With high standards and an insatiable drive to improve, Achievers excel in fields like entrepreneurship, business ownership, sales, marketing, finance, technology, research, and project management. Boring, repetitive tasks? No thank you, they crave challenges that fuel their hunger for progress.

- **Explorers**, the adventurers of the workforce. Driven by curiosity, these bold souls thrive in intellectually stimulating environments where they can push boundaries, solve complex problems, and uncover new frontiers. From research and design to technology, engineering, scientific investigation, and the creative industries, Explorers are the trailblazers of innovation. But beware of stifling routines and uninspiring workplaces—they yearn for the thrill of exploration.

- **Socializers**, the heartbeat of collaboration and human connection, Socializers find their greatest motivation in the rich tapestry of work relationships. They excel in roles that allow them to build connections, network, and communicate effectively. Whether it's in hospitality, marketing, public relations, event planning, teaching, or leadership, they thrive on the energy of interpersonal connections. Solitary work and overly technical positions? They'll pass, craving the lively buzz of social interaction.

- **Challengers**, the adrenaline junkies and competition enthusiasts of the workforce, thrive in high-pressure, high-stakes environments that put their skills and determination to the ultimate test. Whether it's sales, entrepreneurship, law enforcement, military service, competitive sports, or fast-paced industries like trading and investment banking, Challengers are fueled by the thrill of the chase. But beware the mundane and the unchallenging— these warriors yearn for the battlegrounds of excitement.

By considering motivations, work styles, and values alongside skills, we unlock a whole new level of engagement and satisfaction in the workplace. It's time to forge ahead with confidence, celebrating the diverse blend of player types within individuals and unleashing the power within every one of us.

It starts by discovering our player type and then taking small steps toward shaping how we match work to motivations. As we begin to select work, whenever possible, for ourselves and others around us, that best matches the player type, work becomes much less of a drag and more enjoyable. And then, little by little, as we become curious about player types around us, we multiply the power all around. Of course, selecting work might be easier when you are an in-demand freelancer compared to someone who works in an operations role at a bank, but there will be opportunities in most cases. For example, we could volunteer for a project or training that is outside our day-to-day responsibilities' scope but is an excellent match to our player type.

In this brave new world, work becomes a canvas for greatness— a place where witty minds, confident spirits, and captivating talents converge to shape a future that is both engaging and meaningful.

Probability of low compatibility and bad fit

Challengers

In our exploration of game types and their alignment with work preferences, it's essential to recognize that not all roles are well suited to each player type. We will identify the specific categories where certain game types may not find their optimal fit, shedding light on the importance of considering individual inclinations when matching people to work.

Challengers, with their competitive nature and hunger for pushing boundaries, may find themselves at odds with roles that demand strict adherence to rules and procedures. The freedom to compete and explore innovative approaches is vital for Challengers, making environments that restrict autonomy and control less appealing to their innate drive. The structured nature of such roles may dampen their motivation and limit their potential to excel.

Roles involving repetitive or monotonous tasks may also be less than ideal for Challengers. Thriving on challenges that keep them engaged and stimulated, the repetitive nature of certain tasks can lead to boredom and disengagement for Challengers. They crave continuous learning and opportunities to improve their skills, which may not be readily available in roles that lack variety and intellectual stimulation.

Furthermore, Challengers are motivated by the prospect of career advancement and growth. Roles that offer limited room for progression and professional development may not align with their ambitions and drive. Without the opportunity to advance and achieve new milestones, Challengers can become frustrated and disengaged, longing for a more fulfilling career path.

Hybrids

Now, let us explore the concept of hybrid roles, which cater to individuals who do not neatly fit into a single game type. These roles encompass a combination of skills and allow individuals to leverage their diverse strengths.

Creative fields are best suited for those who possess a multifaceted nature that defies categorization. Occupations such as writing, graphic design, music, and film production beckon to individuals with technical skills, originality, and a penchant for innovation. These fields provide an outlet for expressing unique perspectives and ideas, allowing individuals to flourish in their creativity.

Multi-disciplinary roles, which require a broad range of skills and knowledge, can be a fitting choice for those without a dominant player type. Such roles blend creative and analytical skills, often necessitating cooperation with others in a dynamic and collaborative environment. The ability to navigate diverse tasks and adapt to different challenges becomes a valuable asset in these multifaceted positions.

Entrepreneurship, a realm of limitless possibilities, also suits individuals who defy conventional player types. The art of starting and running a business demands a combination of attributes, including creativity, analytical thinking, risk-taking, and effective communication. It offers a unique opportunity for individuals to pursue their passions in a self-directed manner while fostering growth, both personally and professionally.

Types of roles and suitable game types

Sales roles

Now, we shift our focus to sales roles and explore how each game type may find their niche within this field. While Challenger, Achiever, and Explorer personalities can all thrive in sales, the specific types of sales roles that align with their intrinsic motivations and preferences can vary. Let's examine their distinctive inclinations.

Challengers are exceptionally suited for sales roles that embody competition. Industries where salespeople fiercely vie for business or where there is a strong emphasis on meeting and exceeding targets become playgrounds for Challengers to showcase their drive. Consultative or solutions-based selling, where persuading and convincing others are crucial, also aligns with the Challenger's natural skill set.

Achievers, with their goal-oriented nature, thrive in sales roles that offer clear objectives and measurable outcomes. Industries that reward salespeople based on meeting specific targets or goals provide the structure and clarity that fuel the Achiever's desire for progress. Sales roles that facilitate skill-building and offer opportunities for career advancement resonate with their inherent drive for self-improvement and success.

Explorers, driven by curiosity and a thirst for new ideas, excel in sales roles that involve innovation and the exploration of uncharted territories. These roles allow Explorers to push boundaries, bringing fresh perspectives and novel approaches to the sales process. The opportunity for continuous learning and growth in sales environments aligns with the Explorer's desire to acquire new knowledge and refine their skills.

Operational roles

For those seeking their next operations manager, consider the strengths and inclinations of Achievers in this pivotal role. Motivated by the desire to complete tasks and meet goals, Achievers bring a strong work ethic, attention to detail, and a goal-oriented approach to their work.

Operational roles, which involve completing tasks and adhering to established procedures, provide an ideal fit for individuals motivated by meeting targets and driving efficiency.

The realm of operational work encompasses a wide range of roles and industries, including manufacturing, logistics, quality control, and customer service. In these domains, the Achiever's intrinsic desire for structure, organization, and productivity aligns harmoniously with the job requirements. Their ability to work well under pressure and deliver accurate and timely results makes them invaluable assets in roles that demand focused attention to detail and the capacity to operate within tight deadlines.

HR, service, and training

Socializers naturally gravitate to service and training roles because they love human interaction and communication. They find satisfaction in helping others, sharing knowledge, and building relationships. Roles that require empathy, listening, and connecting with others—such as Human Resources, training, customer support, client relationship management, and teaching—would be an excellent fit.

Research and creative

With their endless curiosity and innovative mindset, Explorers excel in research, artistic, and creative roles. They thrive in an environment where they can explore ideas and concepts, express their unique perspective, and push the boundaries of conventional thought and form. Whether in technology companies, or creative think tanks, Explorers will relish the chance to discover, innovate, and create.

Strategy, planning, and investment

Achievers find great enjoyment in roles that require strategic thinking and planning. Their goal-driven nature and attention to detail make them adept at setting clear objectives, devising strategies, and executing plans. Roles in strategic management, business development, consulting, and investments provide the challenge and structured progression that Achievers seek.

Leadership, crisis management, and negotiation

Challengers are competitive and can see opportunities where others see obstacles, making them excellent candidates for positions where they can start and grow businesses, lead transformative change, and forge new paths. These positions demand strong determination, quick thinking, and the ability to take control of high-stakes situations. Whether negotiating complex business deals, managing emergency response teams, or acting as a mediator in conflict resolution, Challengers can excel where the stakes are high and the challenges are complex.

Future roles

Furthermore, we can take a glimpse around the corner of what's possibly coming next in terms of new work.

Achievers will find fulfillment in high-end jobs such as Robotics Engineers, AI and Machine Learning Specialists, Sustainability and Environmental Consultants, and Educational Technology Consultants, where their drive for clear goals and success can truly shine.

Socializers can thrive as Executive Coaches and Leadership Consultants, Human-Machine Interface Designers, or Personalized Nutritionists and Health Coaches, where their innate ability to build relationships and interact with others is critical.

Explorers, driven by curiosity and innovation, may excel as Data Scientists, Virtual Reality (VR) and Augmented Reality (AR) Designers, Quantum Computing Specialists, and Climate Data Analysts exploring new territories and pushing the boundaries of their field.

Challengers are ideally suited for roles as AI and Machine Learning Consultants, Cybersecurity Experts, Advanced-Data Analysts, and Scientists, or 3D Printing Design Specialists, where they can tackle complex problems and challenge the status quo.

Hybrids, who possess a blend of different player traits, can thrive in specialized roles like Content Creators and Strategists, combining aspects of creativity, strategy, and socialization to create unique and meaningful work.

CHAPTER 15
LEVEL 2
SKILLS: TESTING

To be tested is good. The challenged life may be the best therapist.

—Gail Sheehy, author[1]

In our journey to understand the connection between games and intrinsic motivation, we unlock insights into the potential drivers that lie within individuals by testing. These motivations provide a glimpse into their future success in a role. By examining the games individuals play and the reasons they find them exciting, we can uncover their dominant intrinsic motivation and identify their natural drivers.

To apply this understanding to the realm of work, we begin by mapping work tasks to the natural motivations that already exist within those jobs. This alignment ensures a harmonious fit between individuals' intrinsic motivations and the work they engage in. Furthermore, we introduce autonomy within work, allowing team members to select tasks that genuinely interest them rather than forcing them into predefined roles. This empowerment enhances engagement and taps into individuals' natural drivers.

To map out natural motivations that already exist within jobs, we first break down jobs into major tasks that most of the work entails. We then follow that up by identifying the best fit category for each of major tasks:

- **Category 1: Curiosity, Learning, and Innovation.** Task attributes: Research, experimentation, development of new ideas, exploration of new technologies, continuous improvement.

- **Category 2: Achievement, Competence, and Mastery.** Task attributes: Goal-setting, completing projects, meeting targets, acquiring certifications, demonstrating expertise.

- **Category 3: Collaboration, Communication, and Relationship Building.** Task attributes: Teamwork, networking, mentoring, customer interaction, community engagement.

- **Category 4: Competition, Strategy, and Leadership.** Task attributes: Competitive roles, leadership positions, strategic planning, negotiation, conflict resolution.

But how can we make work more fulfilling and game-like without creating full-fledged video games? The answer lies in a simpler and faster alternative: board games. Drawing inspiration from the practices of game houses in Asia, we can build board games that simulate work experiences and gather valuable insights from team members and friends who belong to the potential target segment. By testing these board games, we gain a deeper understanding of the dynamics and emotions that arise as individuals engage with work-related tasks.

Game houses and board game cafés combine the social interaction of cafés with playing board games. They provide a unique space for people to gather, relax, and play a wide variety of board games.

To build a board game that simulates work, we take inspiration from popular board games such as Monopoly, to combine basic elements of competition, decision-making, progress, and chance.

In the attempt to transfer games to the world of work, let's now create a board game that simulates work. See also another invented game in Box 15.1, "Failure to Success: A Workplace Adventure."

We start with setting game objectives. If we are building a game to play out a major business decision, the objective can be to get the most points after one round, as players navigate through the scenarios and consequences of the decision, considering factors such as financial impact, market response, and competition.

A simple linear pathway (can be made into a loop) with alternating squares of opportunity, nothing happens, risk, and challenge, to represent the decision-making process. Distribute an equal number of resource tokens to each player. Decide on a major business decision that the game will revolve around.

Write three simple categories of decision cards, at least five of each, to start thinking through some potential scenarios. The card names can be Opportunities (something good, for example, customers loved your new product, receive 3 tokens), Challenges (something bad, for example, a competitor launches a major sale and your sales drop by a lot, lose 2 tokens), and Risks (could be good or neutral, throw dice to determine if a recent hailstorm damaged a warehouse, if more than 3, deduct the number of tokens).

- **Setup:** Place the player tokens at the starting point of the game board. Shuffle the decision cards and place them in three separate decks.

- **Game play:** each player throws the dice and moves ahead to the number of squares accordingly.

- **Resource tokens:** Representing money, time, and manpower, which players will use to make decisions.

- **Outcome markers:** Indicators to show the results of decisions (e.g., market growth, profit loss).

It's important to note that fun in the context of work is not solely about enjoyable moments. It encompasses the experience of failure and stress, integral components that contribute to growth and resilience. As we design the board game, we pay attention to the signals and emotions it elicits. We strive to create an engaging and enjoyable experience while avoiding aspects that mirror the current state of work—frustration, limitations, and lack of enjoyment. Identifying these undesirable elements allows us to make informed changes and develop a game that captures the essence of work while amplifying its inherent enjoyment.

Feedback mechanisms play a crucial role in this process. Although extrinsic rewards are not the primary focus, feedback serves as a tool for gaging progress and ensuring that we are moving in the right direction. Additionally, we must fine-tune the dynamics of failure (see Box 15.1), balancing the risk of setbacks without discouraging individuals from taking necessary risks. Losing all accumulated progress due to a single failure may create a sense of caution, but we aim to avoid overwhelming feelings of giving up or being stuck.

Within a team setting, we observe a fascinating dynamic related to failure and its impact on team dynamics. When teams collectively lose points due to failure, negative sentiments toward lower performance intensify. Simultaneously, this can lead to aggression toward newcomers, who may be perceived as jeopardizing the team's progress. This behavior is reminiscent of experiences in games like Warcraft, where failure can result in significant losses after hours of collective investment. Understanding this dynamic allows us to design work experiences that align with the desired team behaviors—whether aggressive or supportive—based on the cost and consequences of failure.

Failure, when approached as a learning opportunity, becomes a vital part of the experience. It is crucial to provide clear explanations for failures and indicate how they can be avoided in the future. By incorporating elements of luck and uncertainty into the game—such as using a universal dice—we create a more realistic and relatable simulation of the real world.

Game designers employ various methods to identify and eliminate boring elements from games. Play-testing allows designers to observe how players interact with the game and identify areas that need improvement. User feedback, gathered through surveys, focus groups, and player forums, provides valuable insights into players' experiences and helps identify enjoyable and boring aspects of the game. Data analysis enables designers to track player behavior and engagement, identify patterns, and make informed changes to enhance enjoyment.

Designers may also create user personas that represent the target audience, enabling them to make decisions based on the preferences and motivations of these fictional characters. Finally, game design is an iterative process, with incremental changes made to refine and improve the game until it reaches its maximum enjoyment potential.

By applying these principles and methods to the realm of work, we can craft experiences that tap into individuals' intrinsic motivations, enhance engagement, and elevate the enjoyment and fulfillment derived from their professional pursuits.

For example, the team introduces a feedback loop inspired by game play-testing. After each project iteration, the team gathers user feedback, analyses engagement patterns, and identifies areas for improvement. By embracing failures as learning opportunities and continually fine-tuning the process, they enhance the user experience, align their work with user preferences, and create a more resilient and adaptive development process.

Or a customer support team identifies the tedious task of repetitive data entry as a demotivating factor. They simulate their daily workflow as a game, including the mundane data entry task. By having team members and others play this simulated game and provide feedback, they pinpoint the least engaging aspects. Through continuous refinement and implementing of technological solutions, they successfully eliminated the tedious data entry component, allowing the team to focus on more exciting tasks and increasing the feeling of control.

Box 15.1 Game: "Failure to Success: A Workplace Adventure"

In our quest to transform work into a game-like experience, we introduce "Failure to Success: A Workplace Adventure," a game that aims to instill in players the understanding that failure is an integral part of work and can serve as a stepping stone to success. Through this game, players will learn how to approach failure with a positive attitude, embrace the lessons it offers, and discover ways to bounce back and grow from their experiences.

- **Game play:** The game board is divided into a series of squares, each representing different stages of a typical work project. Players take turns rolling a dice and moving their game piece along the board, simulating the progression of a real work endeavor.

- **Challenges:** At each stage, players encounter various challenges that can either be positive or negative experiences. These challenges mirror the unpredictability and uncertainties of the workplace. For instance, players might receive positive feedback from a boss, boosting their confidence and progress. Conversely, they might face setbacks that require them to reevaluate their approach and start anew.

- **Failure:** Landing on a square labeled "failure" prompts players to draw a card that presents them with a specific failure scenario. The card guides them to reflect on a past failure and consider the valuable

(Continued)

lessons learned from it. Alternatively, it may encourage players to contemplate how they can leverage their current setback as an opportunity for growth and development.

- **Reflection:** After each turn, players are encouraged to engage in reflective discussions with the group. This allows them to share their experiences, delve into their emotions, and articulate the lessons they have learned from their encounters. By fostering open dialogue, players can gain insights from another's perspective and broaden their understanding of failure's transformative potential.

- **Points:** The game incorporates a points system to incentivize positive behaviors and attitudes. Players earn points for actions that demonstrate resilience, such as seeking feedback from coworkers or turning a failure into a valuable learning opportunity. Additionally, points are awarded for displaying a positive attitude, such as offering encouragement to fellow players or showcasing unwavering determination in the face of adversity.

- **Endgame:** The game concludes when all players have completed the project and reached the end of the board. At this point, the player with the highest number of points emerges as the victor. The endgame underscores the importance of persevering through challenges, embracing failure as a catalyst for growth, and embodying the qualities that lead to success in the workplace.

"Failure to Success: A Workplace Adventure" serves as a powerful tool for transforming individuals' perceptions of failure and nurturing a resilient mindset within the context of work. Through engaging gameplay, reflective discussions, and the pursuit of points, players are equipped with the skills and mindset needed to turn setbacks into stepping stones on their path to success.

Note

1. Gail Sheehy, *Passages: Predictable Crises of Adult Life* (New York: Dutton, 1976).

CHAPTER 16
LEVEL 3 SKILLS: AND THE FUTURE OF WORK IS. . .

The digital economy has become an increasingly significant contributor to global GDP, with the internet economy growing at an astonishing pace. As we embark on the next phase of technological advances, we are on the verge of a transformative era that will redefine the way we work. At the heart of this groundbreaking technology lies a term that may have seemed like a passing trend but is now poised to revolutionize numerous industries: blockchain.

I must admit that, in the early days, I was among the skeptics who questioned the potential of blockchain. The space was rife with dubious activities and characterized by a Wild West mentality. However, over time, I have come to recognize the immense value and potential that blockchain offers.

So, what exactly is blockchain? At its core, a blockchain is a digital ledger used to record information or transactions. It operates in the same way as a traditional ledger or spreadsheet but differs in that it is decentralized and distributed across multiple computers. This decentralization ensures that there is no single point of control or failure, making blockchain highly secure and resistant to tampering.

Imagine a chain of digital blocks, with each block containing a record of something significant. Once a new transaction or piece of information is added to a block, it becomes an immutable part of the chain. This permanence and immutability create a transparent and unchangeable record of all transactions conducted on the blockchain, visible to all participants within the network.

The potential applications of blockchain are vast and varied. It can be used for creating digital currencies, tracking products throughout the supply chain, managing digital identities, and much more. Essentially, it functions as a digital version of a public record book, visible to all but impervious to alteration.

In terms of accessibility and control, there are two main types of blockchains: public and private. Public blockchains are decentralized networks open to anyone, not controlled by a single entity. They are typically permissionless, enabling anyone to participate, read data, and even create new blocks. Prominent examples of public blockchains include Bitcoin and Ethereum.

In contrast, private blockchains are controlled by a single organization or a consortium of entities. These networks are usually closed, granting access exclusively to authorized individuals or organizations. Private blockchains are typically permissioned, allowing only authorized participants to access and modify the data. Notable examples of private blockchains include Hyperledger, Corda, and Quorum.

Public blockchains emphasize transparency, security, and decentralization, making them suitable for use cases that require openness to the public, such as digital currencies. Private blockchains, on the other hand, prioritize control and privacy, making them more suitable for enterprise solutions, supply chain management, and healthcare applications.

Web3, also known as the decentralized web or blockchain web, represents the next evolution of the internet. The current iteration, Web2, relies on centralized systems controlled by a small number of large corporations and organizations. Web3, however, is built on decentralized systems like blockchain, enabling a more distributed and democratic internet.

A key feature of Web3 is the utilization of decentralized networks, such as blockchain, to power web applications. This facilitates the development of decentralized applications (dApps) that operate independently, free from the control of any single entity. Web3 fosters a more open, transparent, and secure internet, where users retain greater control over their data, liberated from the grip of centralized organizations.

Furthermore, Web3 enables the establishment of decentralized autonomous organizations (DAOs), where decision-making is driven by the community rather than a central authority. This democratic and transparent approach can lead to more efficient and equitable systems.

Web3 technologies also facilitate the creation of digital assets and smart contracts, which represent real-world assets like property, art, and stocks. These assets can be transferred and traded in a trustless and transparent manner, revolutionizing traditional financial systems. A trustless system means that users don't have to trust a central authority, a third party, or even each other to engage in transactions or interactions. This is a key foundation for the crypto and blockchain economy.

Although Web3 is still in its early stages, and the decentralized web has yet to be widely adopted, the momentum behind this movement is undeniable. Blockchain technology is already

THE POWER OF PLAY

being harnessed across various sectors, ranging from finance to supply chain management, signaling a promising future.

As we envision the future of work, it is crucial to recognize the potential impact of blockchains and Web3. These technologies offer new possibilities for transparency, trust, and collaboration. They empower individuals, challenge traditional power structures, and pave the way for a more inclusive and equitable work landscape.

In this brave new world, the boundaries between work and play blur, and the power of gamification merges with the transformative force of blockchain.

DAO: revolutionizing collaboration and governance

In the realm of blockchain technology, a new paradigm of organization has emerged—the decentralized autonomous organization, or DAO. These digital entities operate on blockchain networks and are governed by their members through smart contracts, encoding rules that define their operation. DAOs are a profound departure from traditional centralized organizations, as they distribute power and decision-making authority among their members, fostering a decentralized and trustless environment.

In a "trustless" system like DAO, you don't need to trust people or organizations because the blockchain technology itself makes sure everything is fair and honest for everyone.

The fundamental purpose of a DAO is to enable individuals to come together and collaborate toward a shared objective in a transparent and open manner. These organizations serve a wide range of purposes, from facilitating decentralized finance to supporting online communities and decentralized marketplaces. By leveraging the power of blockchain technology, DAOs offer unprecedented transparency, immutability, and security.

DAOs embody the principles of openness and inclusivity, allowing anyone to access and review the rules and proposals that govern the organization. Furthermore, participation in decision-making is not limited to a select few; rather, it is open to all members of the DAO. Consensus mechanisms, such as voting, ensure that proposals are collectively decided upon, ensuring that the interests of the community are upheld.

The connection between DAOs and the gamification of work is the transparent, collaborative, and incentivized nature of both. DAOs represent a new paradigm of organization that operates on decentralized blockchain networks, distributing power and decision-making authority among its members. This creates an environment that fosters collaboration, incentivizes active participation, and aligns personal and collective interests. DAOs blur the lines between work and games.

It is worth noting that despite the term "autonomous" in its name, a DAO's control is not entirely autonomous. Smart contracts, which dictate the functioning of a DAO, are written by humans and are subject to bugs or security vulnerabilities. However, through careful design and continuous improvement, DAOs strive to minimize risks and create robust systems.

Members of a DAO are incentivized through a variety of mechanisms embedded within the organization's smart contract infrastructure. These incentives motivate active participation, alignment of interests, and adherence to the rules and objectives of the DAO. Let's explore some common incentives employed by DAOs:

- **Rewards for participating in decision-making:** Members receive rewards for actively engaging in the decision-making process, voting on proposals, and shaping the direction of the organization. These rewards often take the form of tokens or cryptocurrency, which can be used within the DAO ecosystem or traded on open markets.

- **Financial incentives:** DAOs managing financial assets, such as decentralized funds, provide members with incentives tied to the fund's performance. Members may receive a share of the profits or revenue generated by the fund, encouraging active involvement and contribution to its success.

- **Reputation-based incentives:** In a DAO, reputation plays a crucial role in influencing decision-making. Members gain reputation by actively participating, demonstrating expertise, and contributing positively to the organization. Increased reputation can enhance the weight of their vote on proposals or unlock additional benefits and privileges.

- **Penalties for non-participation:** To ensure active engagement, DAOs may impose penalties for non-participation or non-compliance with the organization's rules. Penalties can range from reputation loss to restricted access to benefits or, in extreme cases, exclusion from decision-making processes.

- **Alignment of interests:** DAOs are designed to align the interests of their members with the collective goals of the organization. By ensuring that personal gains and the success of the DAO are intertwined, individuals are incentivized to act in the best interest of the organization as a whole.

The rise of DAOs signifies a profound shift in the way organizations function, embracing decentralization, transparency, and community-driven decision-making. As these entities continue to evolve, they hold the potential to revolutionize collaboration, governance, and the very fabric of our socio-economic systems. By empowering individuals and fostering a sense of ownership, DAOs pave the way for a more inclusive, equitable, and resilient future of work.

Thanks for coming on this journey of discovering the power of play. We found out that the future of work is fun, it is enjoyable, it is engaging, and it is closer than we thought. Now it is your turn to take the controller and make tomorrow's work your game. Be a winner, and let's unleash the power of play at work!

ABOUT THE AUTHOR

Hailing from Canada and leaving his mark across the vibrant landscapes of Asia, George is a successful entrepreneur celebrated for his breakthrough innovations. His formidable journey traces back to a thriving career in the financial services industry spanning the breadth of Asia, which eventually led him to the dynamic world of fintech ventures.

The founder of a prestigious regional association and an acquired startup, George emerged as a thought leader in this rapidly evolving field. As the Chief Commercial Officer of a pioneering technology firm—backed by the world's preeminent online insurance provider and a formidable consortium of investors—George was instrumental in propelling the company's sales, doubling them across Asia.

With an infectious passion for sharing his knowledge, George is a regular contributor to global publications and a sought-after speaker at prestigious events. Furthermore, his insights can be found in *The InsurTech Book*, which he co-authored, published by John Wiley & Sons in 2018. Outside the world of technology and innovation, George cherishes family moments in Singapore. He holds an MBA from the University of Western Ontario, Canada.

ABOUT THE BOOK

In the quest to understand the universal allure of games, this book ventures into the realm of game design, investigating its potential to make work not just tolerable but enjoyable and rewarding for all. The sad truth is that, for most people, work—where we spend the majority of our lives—has become a burdensome chore. Through a unique blend of research and riveting narratives, this book delves into the root causes of work dissatisfaction, underlining the outdated systems in place and offering insights from the world of games as a promising solution.

Did you know that the average individual indulges in games for approximately 8.5 hours per week? Despite slight cultural variations, people globally dedicate nearly a full day each week to this delightful escape of problem-solving. Interestingly, the myriad games we enjoy seem to align with a few core categories that tap into our deepest motivations—motivations that are enduring and trace back to our childhood.

Our exploration led to a striking revelation. Unraveling the games you loved as a child could be the key to uncovering your profound motivations and identifying the most fulfilling work for you. The parallel between games and work is strong—both involve creative problem-solving and deep concentration. Games, however, offer us control, allowing us to switch when boredom creeps in. Our attraction to games is partly due to this freedom and partly due to the clever design and alignment with our core motivations, ultimately leading us to a state of flow.

The COVID-19 pandemic and its dramatic upheaval of conventional work routines allowed people worldwide to experience freedom of work choice on an unprecedented scale. This newfound autonomy sparked a global rebellion against factory-style work, manifested in waves of mass resignations followed by a job market reshuffle. The lesson is clear—we must transform work into an engaging, enjoyable experience or risk a precipitous decline in productivity and economic stagnation.

Unfortunately, gamification alone is insufficient, as it often overlooks our individualistic needs and motivations. A one-size-fits-all strategy is bound to fail—imagine a tennis lover confined to a slot machine for years; the dissatisfaction would be palpable.

This book addresses these critical pain points and opportunities to enhance work engagement. It provides actionable insights into tapping into intrinsic motivations and fostering a more satisfying work experience.

ACKNOWLEDGMENTS

I want to take a moment to express my deepest gratitude to the incredible individuals who have contributed their ideas, insights, and precious time to bring this book to life. Writing a book is like embarking on an adventure, and I am forever grateful for the unwavering support and collaboration of these remarkable people.

First and foremost, I want to give a big shoutout to Chris Wei, my guiding light in this journey. Chris, your patient guidance and steadfast belief in the potential of this book have been nothing short of extraordinary. Your wisdom and thought-provoking questions have pushed me to dig deeper, challenge my own assumptions, and refine my ideas. I am truly indebted to you for your invaluable contributions and mentorship.

A special heartfelt thanks goes to the incredible team at Wiley, especially Annie Knight. I can't thank you enough for believing in my pitch and guiding me through this exciting process. Your expertise, patience, and dedication have been a beacon of light on this rollercoaster ride. I am grateful for the countless hours you've invested in turning my vision into a reality. You have made this dream come true.

ACKNOWLEDGMENTS

To my extraordinary wife, you are the wind beneath my wings. Your unwavering support, love, and understanding have carried me through the highs and lows of writing this book. You created a sacred space for me to dive into my thoughts, shielding me from the distractions of daily life and allowing my creativity to flow freely. I am forever grateful for your belief in me and this project.

A heartfelt shoutout to my dear friends, the unsung heroes of this journey. You patiently listened to my endless rants, passionate monologues, and crazy ideas about the future of work. Your feedback, encouragement, and honest conversations have breathed life into the ideas presented in this book. Your support and friendship have been a constant source of inspiration. I cherish each and every one of you.

And to you, my dear readers, I want to express my deepest gratitude. Thank you for embarking on this adventure with me. Your curiosity, engagement, and support give purpose and meaning to the words written on these pages. It is my sincerest hope that this book sparks inspiration, ignites conversations, and offers valuable insights as we navigate the ever-changing landscape of work together.

INDEX

INDEX